THE BOOK OF AMERICAN
NEGRO SPIRITUALS

THE BOOK OF AMERICAN NEGRO SPIRITUALS

Edited with an introduction by
JAMES WELDON JOHNSON

Musical arrangements by
J. ROSAMOND JOHNSON

Additional numbers by
LAWRENCE BROWN

NEW YORK   THE VIKING PRESS   MCMXXV

MANUFACTURED IN THE UNITED STATES OF AMERICA
BY THE VAIL-BALLOU PRESS, INC., BINGHAMTON, N. Y.

Printing Statement:

Due to the very old age and scarcity of this book,
many of the pages may be hard to read due to the
blurring of the original text, possible missing pages,
missing text and other issues beyond our control.

Because this is such an important and rare work, we
believe it is best to reproduce this book regardless of
its original condition.

Thank you for your understanding.

To those through whose efforts these
songs have been collected, preserved
and given to the world this book
is lovingly dedicated.

CONTENTS

CONTENTS

THE BOOK OF AMERICAN
NEGRO SPIRITUALS

PREFACE

O BLACK AND UNKNOWN BARDS

O black and unknown bards of long ago,
How came your lips to touch the sacred fire?
How, in your darkness, did you come to know
The power and beauty of the minstrel's lyre?
Who first from midst his bonds lifted his eyes?
Who first from out the still watch, lone and long,
Feeling the ancient faith of prophets rise
Within his dark-kept soul, burst into song?

Heart of what slave poured out such melody
As "Steal away to Jesus"?   On its strains
His spirit must have nightly floated free,
Though still about his hands he felt his chains.
Who heard great "Jordan roll"?   Whose starward eye
Saw chariot "swing low"?   And who was he
That breathed that comforting, melodic sigh,
"Nobody knows de trouble I see"?

What merely living clod, what captive thing,
Could up toward God through all its darkness grope,
And find within its deadened heart to sing
These songs of sorrow, love and faith, and hope?
How did it catch that subtle undertone,
That note in music heard not with the ears?
How sound the elusive reed so seldom blown,
Which stirs the soul or melts the heart to tears?

Not that great German master in his dream
Of harmonies that thundered amongst the stars
At the creation, ever heard a theme
Nobler than "Go down, Moses."   Mark its bars,
How like a mighty trumpet call they stir

PREFACE

The blood. Such are the notes that men have sung
Going to valorous deeds; such tones there were
That helped make history when time was young.

There is a wide, wide wonder in it all,
That from degraded rest and servile toil
The fiery spirit of the seer should call
These simple children of the sun and soil.
O black slave singers, gone forgot, unfamed,
You—you alone, of all the long, long line
Of those who've sung untaught, unknown, unnamed,
Have stretched out upward, seeking the divine.
You sang not deeds of heroes or of kings;

No chant of bloody war, no exulting pæan
Of arms-won triumphs; but your humble strings
You touched in chord with music empyrean.
You sang far better than you knew; the songs
That for your listeners' hungry hearts sufficed
Still live,—but more than this to you belongs:
You sang a race from wood and stone to Christ.

It was in the above lines, which appeared in the *Century Magazine* nearly twenty years ago, that I tried to voice my estimate and appreciation of the Negro Spirituals and to celebrate the unknown black bards who created them. As the years go by and I understand more about this music and its origin the miracle of its production strikes me with increasing wonder. It would have been a notable achievement if the white people who settled this country, having a common language and heritage, seeking liberty in a new land, faced with the task of conquering untamed nature, and stirred with the hope of building an empire, had created a body of folk music comparable to the Negro Spirituals. But from whom did these songs spring—these songs unsurpassed among the folk songs of the world and, in the poignancy of their beauty, unequalled?

In 1619 a Dutch vessel landed twenty African natives at Jamestown, Virginia. They were quickly bought up by the colonial settlers. This was the beginning of the African slave trade in the American Colonies. To supply this trade Africa was raped of millions of men, women and

12

children. [1] As many as survived the passage were immediately thrown into slavery. These people came from various localities in Africa. They did not all speak the same language. Here they were, suddenly cut off from the moorings of their native culture, scattered without regard to their old tribal relations, having to adjust themselves to a completely alien civilization, having to learn a strange language, and, moreover, held under an increasingly harsh system of slavery; yet it was from these people this mass of noble music sprang; this music which is America's only folk music and, up to this time, the finest distinctive artistic contribution she has to offer the world. It is strange!

I have termed this music noble, and I do so without any qualifications. Take, for example, *Go Down, Moses;* there is not a nobler theme in the whole musical literature of the world. If the Negro had voiced himself in only that one song, it would have been evidence of his nobility of soul. Add to this *Deep River, Stand Still Jordan, Walk Together Children, Roll Jordan Roll, Ride On King Jesus,* and you catch a spirit that is a little more than mere nobility; it is something akin to majestic grandeur. The music of these songs is always noble and their sentiment is always exalted. Never does their philosophy fall below the highest and purest motives of the heart. And this might seem stranger still.

Perhaps there will be no better point than this at which to say that all the true Spirituals possess dignity. It is, of course, pardonable to smile at the naïveté often exhibited in the words, but it should be remembered that in scarcely no instance was anything humorous intended. When it came to the use of words, the maker of the song was struggling as best he could under his limitations in language and, perhaps, also under a misconstruction or misapprehension of the facts in his source of material, generally the Bible. And often, like his more literary poetic brothers, he had to do a good many things to get his rhyme in. But almost always he was in dead earnest. There are doubtless many persons who have heard these songs sung only on the vaudeville or theatrical stage and have laughed uproariously at them because they were presented in humorous vein. Such people

[1] For a history of the slave trade and its horrors see "The Suppression of the Slave Trade" by W. E. B. Du Bois.

have no conception of the Spirituals. They probably thought of them as a new sort of ragtime or minstrel song. These Spirituals cannot be properly appreciated or understood unless they are clothed in their primitive dignity.

No space will here be given to a rehearsal of the familiar or easily accessible facts regarding the origin and development of folk music in general. Nor will any attempt be made at a discussion of the purely technical questions of music involved. A thorough exposition of this latter phase of the subject will be found in H. E. Krehbiel's *Afro-American Folksongs*. There Mr. Krehbiel makes an analysis of the modes, scales and intervals of these songs and a comparative study between them and the same features of other folksongs. Here it is planned, rather, to relate regarding these songs as many facts as possible that will be of interest to the general lover of music and serve to present adequately this collection. Instead of dissecting this music we hope to recreate around it as completely as we can its true atmosphere and place it in a proper setting for those who already love the Spirituals and those who may come to know them.

✗ Although the Spirituals have been overwhelmingly accredited to the Negro as his own, original creation, nevertheless, there have been one or two critics who have denied that they were original either with the Negro or in themselves, and a considerable number of people have eagerly accepted this view. The opinion of these critics is not sound. It is not based upon scientific or historical inquiry. Indeed, it can be traced ultimately to a prejudiced attitude of mind, to an unwillingness to concede the creation of so much pure beauty to a people they wish to feel is absolutely inferior. Once that power is conceded, the idea of absolute inferiority cannot hold. These critics point to certain similarities in structure between the Spirituals and the folk music of other peoples, ignoring the fact that there are such similarities between all folksongs. The Negro Spirituals are as distinct from the folksongs of other peoples as those songs are from each other; and, perhaps, more so. One needs to be only ordinarily familiar with the folk music of the world to see that this is so.

14

PREFACE

The statement that the Spirituals are imitations made by the Negro of other music that he heard is an absurdity. What music did American Negroes hear to imitate? They certainly had no opportunity to go to Scotland or Russia or Scandinavia and bring back echoes of songs from those lands. Some of them may have heard a few Scotch songs in this country, but it is inconceivable that this great mass of five or six hundred Negro songs could have sprung from such a source. What music then was left for them to imitate? Some have gone so far as to say that they caught snatches of airs from the French Opera at New Orleans; but the songs of the Negroes who fell most directly under that influence are of a type distinct from the Spirituals. It was in localities far removed from New Orleans that the great body of Spirituals were created and sung. There remains then the music which the American Negroes heard their masters sing; chiefly religious music. Now if ignorant Negroes evolved such music as *Deep River, Steal Away to Jesus, Somebody's Knockin' at Yo' Do', I Couldn't Hear Nobody Pray* and *Father Abraham* by listening to their masters sing gospel hymns, it does not detract from the achievement but magnifies it.

Regarding the origin of this music, I myself have referred to the "miracle" of its production. And it is easier to believe the miracle than some of the explanations of it that are offered. Most difficult of all is it to believe that the Negro slaves were indebted to their white masters for the sources of these songs. The white people among whom the slaves lived did not originate anything comparable even to the mere titles of the Spirituals. In truth, the power to frame the poetic phrases that make the titles of so many of the Spirituals betokens the power to create the songs. Consider the sheer magic of:

Swing Low Sweet Chariot
I've Got to Walk My Lonesome Valley
Steal Away to Jesus
Singing With a Sword in My Hand
Rule Death in His Arms
Ride on King Jesus
We Shall Walk Through the Valley in Peace
The Blood Came Twinklin' Down

15

PREFACE

Deep River
Death's Goin' to Lay His Cold, Icy Hand on Me

and confess that none but an artistically endowed people could have evoked it.

No one has even expressed a doubt that the poetry of the titles and text of the Spirituals is Negro in character and origin, no one else has dared to lay claim to it; why then doubt the music? There is a slight analogy here to the Shakespeare-Bacon controversy. The Baconians in their amazement before the transcendent greatness of the plays declare that Shakespeare could not possibly have written them; he was not scholar enough; he did not know enough Greek; no mere play actor could be gentleman enough to be so familiar with the ways of the court and royalty; no mere play actor could be philosopher enough to know all the hidden springs of human motives and conduct. Then they pick a man who fills these requirements and accounts for the phenomenon of the crowning glory of the English tongue. Lord Francis Bacon, they say, wrote the plays but did not claim them because it was not creditable for a gentleman to be a playwright. However, though it was creditable for a gentleman of the age to be a poet, they do not explain why Lord Bacon did not claim the poems. And it is easy to see that the hand that wrote the poems could write the plays.

Nobody thought of questioning the Negro's title as creator of this music until its beauty and value were demonstrated. The same thing, in a greater degree, has transpired with regard to the Negro as the originator of America's popular medium of musical expression; in fact, to such a degree that it is now completely divorced from all ideas associated with the Negro. Still, for several very good reasons, it will not be easy to do that with the Spirituals.

When the Fisk Jubilee Singers [2] toured Europe they sang in England, Scotland and Germany, spending eight months in the latter country. Their concerts were attended by the most cultured and so-

---

[2] The Jubilee Singers of Fisk University first introduced the Spirituals to the public. From 1871 to 1875 they gave many concerts in the United States. and made two tours of Europe. They raised a net sum of more than $150,000 for the University. Jubilee Hall is one of the monuments of their efforts.

16

PREFACE

phisticated people as well as the general public. In England they
sang before Queen Victoria, and in Germany the Emperor was among
those who listened to them. Music critics paid special attention to the
singers and their songs. The appearance of the Jubilee Singers in
Europe constituted both an artistic sensation and a financial success,
neither of which results could have been attained had their songs been
mere imitations of European folk music or adaptations of European
airs.

The Spirituals are purely and solely the creation of the American
Negro; that is, as much so as any music can be the pure and sole
creation of any particular group. And their production, although
seemingly miraculous, can be accounted for naturally. The Negro
brought with him from Africa his native musical instinct and talent,
and that was no small endowment to begin with.

Many things are now being learned about Africa. It is being learned
and recognized that the great majority of Africans are in no sense
"savages"; that they possess a civilization and a culture, primitive
it is true but in many respects quite adequate; that they possess a
folk literature that is varied and rich; that they possess an art that is
quick and sound. Among those who know about art it is generally
recognized that the modern school of painting and sculpture in Europe
and America is almost entirely the result of the direct influence of
African art, following the discovery that it was art.[3] Not much is
yet known about African music, and, perhaps, for the reason that the
conception of music by the Africans is not of the same sort as the
conception of music by the people of Western Europe and the United

[3] "Of all the arts of the primitive races, the art of the African Negro savage is the one
which has had a positive influence upon the art of our epoch. From its principles of plastic
representation a new art movement has evolved. The point of departure and the resting point
of our abstract representation are based on the art of that race. It is certain that before the
introduction of the plastic principles of Negro art, abstract representations did not exist
among Europeans. Negro art has reawakened in us the feeling for abstract form; it has
brought into our art the means to express our purely sensorial feelings in regard to form, or
to find new form in our ideas. The abstract representation of modern art is unquestionably
the offspring of the Negro Art, which has made us conscious of the subjective state, ob-
literated by objective education." *African Negro Art—Its Influence on Modern Art*, M. de
Zayas.

17

PREFACE

States. Generally speaking, the European concept of music is melody and the African concept is rhythm. Melody has, relatively, small place in African music, and harmony still less; but in rhythms African music is beyond comparison with any other music in the world. Krehbiel, after visiting the Dahomey Village at the World's Fair in Chicago, and witnessing the natives dance to the accompaniment of choral singing and the beating of their drums, wrote of them:

"The players showed the most remarkable rhythmical sense and skill that ever came under my notice. Berlioz, in his supremest effort with his army of drummers, produced nothing to compare in artistic interest with the harmonious drumming of these savages. The fundamental effect was a combination of double and triple time, the former kept by the singers, the latter by the drummers, but it is impossible to convey the idea of the wealth of detail achieved by the drummers by means of exchange of the rhythms, syncopation of both simultaneously, and dynamic devices. Only by making a score of the music could this be done. I attempted to make such a score by enlisting the help of the late John C. Fillmore, experienced in Indian music, but we were thwarted by the players who, evidently divining our purpose when we took out our notebooks, mischievously changed their manner of playing as soon as we touched pencil to paper. I was forced to the conclusion that in their command of the element, which in the musical art of the ancient Greeks stood higher than either melody or harmony, the best composers of today were the veriest tyros compared with these black savages." [4]

The musical genius of the African has not become so generally recognized as his genius in sculpture and design, and yet it has had a wide influence on the music of the world. Friedenthal points out that African Negroes have a share in the creation of one of the best known and most extended musical forms, the Habanera.[5] This form which is popularly known as the chief characteristic of Spanish music is a combination of Spanish melody and African rhythm. Friedenthal, regarding this combination, says:

Here stand these two races facing each other, both highly musical but reared in different worlds of music. Little wonder that the Spaniards quickly took

[4] H. E. Krehbiel, *Afro-American Folksongs.* New York, 1914.
[5] Alfred Friedenthal, *Stimmen der Völker.* Berlin, 1911.

18

advantage of these remarkable rhythms and incorporated them into their own music. . . . The melody of the Habanera came out of Middle or Southern Spain, and the rhythm which accompanies it had its origin in Africa. We therefore have, in a way, the union of Spanish spirit and African technique." [6]

The rhythm of the Habanera reduced to its simplest is:

and is the rhythm characteristic of Spanish and Latin-American music. A considerable portion of Bizet's opera, Carmen, is based on this originally African rhythm.

Further, regarding the musical genius of the Africans, Friedenthal says: "Now the African Negroes possess great musical talent. It must be admitted, though, that in the invention of melodies, they do not come up to the European standard, but the greater is their capacity as inventors of rhythms. The talent exhibited by the Bantus in contriving the most complex rhythms is nothing short of marvelous." [7]

Now, the Negro in America had his native musical endowment to begin with; and the Spirituals possess the fundamental characteristics of African music. They have a striking rhythmic quality, and show a marked similarity to African songs in form and intervallic structure. But the Spirituals, upon the base of the primitive rhythms, go a step in advance of African music through a higher melodic and an added harmonic development. For the Spirituals are not merely melodies. The melodies of many of them, so sweet or strong or even weird, are wonderful, but hardly more wonderful than the harmonies. One has never experienced the full effect of these songs until he has heard their harmonies in the part singing of a large number of Negro voices. I shall say more about this question of harmony later. But what led to this advance by the American Negro beyond his primitive music? Why did he not revive and continue the beating out of complex rhythms on tom toms and drums while he uttered barbaric and martial cries to

[6] Alfred Friedenthal, *Musik, Tanz und Dichtung bei den Kreolen Amerikas.*
[7] Alfred Friedenthal, *Stimmen der Völker.* Berlin, 1911.

19

PREFACE

their accompaniment? It was because at the precise and psychic moment there was blown through or fused into the vestiges of his African music the spirit of Christianity as he knew Christianity.

At the psychic moment there was at hand the precise religion for the condition in which he found himself thrust. Far from his native land and customs, despised by those among whom he lived, experiencing the pang of the separation of loved ones on the auction block, knowing the hard task master, feeling the lash, the Negro seized Christianity, the religion of compensations in the life to come for the ills suffered in the present existence, the religion which implied the hope that in the next world there would be a reversal of conditions, of rich man and poor man, of proud and meek, of master and slave. The result was a body of songs voicing all the cardinal virtues of Christianity—patience—forbearance—love—faith—and hope—through a necessarily modified form of primitive African music. The Negro took complete refuge in Christianity, and the Spirituals were literally forged of sorrow in the heat of religious fervor. They exhibited, moreover, a reversion to the simple principles of primitive, communal Christianity.

The thought that the Negro might have refused or failed to adopt Christianity—and there were several good reasons for such an outcome, one being the vast gulf between the Christianity that was preached to him and the Christianity practiced by those who preached it—leads to some curious speculations. One thing is certain, there would have been no Negro Spirituals. His musical instinct would doubtless have manifested itself; but is it conceivable that he could have created a body of songs in any other form so unique in the musical literature of the world and with such a powerful and universal appeal as the Spirituals? Indeed, the question arises, would he have been able to survive slavery in the way in which he did? It is not possible to estimate the sustaining influence that the story of the trials and tribulations of the Jews as related in the Old Testament exerted upon the Negro. This story at once caught and fired the imaginations of the Negro bards, and they sang, sang their hungry listeners into a firm faith that as God saved Daniel in the lion's den, so would He save them; as God preserved the Hebrew children in the fiery furnace, so would He preserve them; as God delivered Israel out of bondage in Egypt, so would He deliver them. How much this firm faith had to do with the Negro's physical and spiritual survival of two and a half centuries of slavery cannot be known.

Thus it was by sheer spiritual forces that African chants were metamorphosed into the Spirituals; that upon the fundamental throb of African rhythms were reared those reaches of melody that rise above earth and soar into the pure, ethereal blue. And this is the miracle of the creation of the Spirituals.

As is true of all folksongs, there are two theories as to the manner in which the Spirituals were "composed"; whether they were the spontaneous outburst and expression of the group or chiefly the work of individual talented makers. I doubt that either theory is exclusively correct. The Spirituals are true folksongs and originally intended only for group singing. Some of them may be the spontaneous creation of the group, but my opinion is that the far greater part of them is the work of talented individuals influenced by the pressure and reaction of the group. The responses, however, may be more largely the work of the group in action; it is likely that they simply burst forth. It is also true that many of these songs have been modified and varied as they have been sung by different groups in different localities. This process is still going on. Sometimes we find two or more distinct variations of the melody of a song. There are also the interchange and substitution of lines. Yet, it is remarkable that these variations and changes are as few as they are, considering the fact that these songs have been for generations handed down from ear to ear and by word of mouth. Variations in melody are less common than interchange of lines. The committing to memory of all the leading lines constituted quite a feat, for they run high into the hundreds; so sometimes the leader's memory failed him and he would have to improvise or substitute. This substituting accounts for a good deal of the duplication of leading lines.

In the old days there was a definitely recognized order of bards, and to some degree it still persists. These bards gained their recognition by achievement. They were makers of songs and leaders of singing. They had to possess certain qualifications: a gift of melody, a talent for poetry, a strong voice, and a good memory. Here we have a demand for a great many gifts in one individual; yet, they were all necessary. The recognized bard required the ability to make up the appealing tune, to fashion the graphic phrase, to pitch the tune true and lead it clearly, and to remember all the lines. There was, at least, one leader of singing in every congregation but makers of songs were less common. My memory of childhood goes back to a great leader of singing, "Ma" White, and a maker of songs, "Singing" Johnson. "Ma" White was an excellent laundress and a busy woman, but each church meeting found her in her place ready to lead the singing, whenever the formal choir and organ did not usurp her ancient rights. I can still recall her shrill, plaintive voice quavering above the others. Memory distinctly brings back her singing of *We Are Climbing Jacob's Ladder, Keep Me From Sinking Down*, and *We Shall Walk Through the Valley in Peace*. Even as a child my joy in hearing her sing these songs was deep and full. She was the recognized leader of spiritual singing in the congregation to which she belonged and she took her duties seriously. One of her duties was to "sing-down" a long-winded or uninteresting speaker at love feasts or experience meetings, and even to cut short a prayer of undue length by raising a song. (And what a gentle method of gaining relief from a tiresome speaker. Why shouldn't it be generally adopted today?) "Ma" White had a great reputation as a leader of singing, a reputation of which she was proud and jealous. She knew scores of Spirituals, but I do not think she ever "composed" any songs.

On the other hand, singing was "Singing" Johnson's only business. He was not a fixture in any one congregation or community, but went from one church to another, singing his way. I can recall that his periodical visits caused a flutter of excitement akin to that caused by the visit of a famed preacher. These visits always meant the hearing and learning of something new. I recollect how the congregation would hang on his voice for a new song—new, at least to them. They listened through, some of them joining in waveringly. The quicker ears soon caught the melody and words. The whole congregation easily learned the response, which is generally unvarying. They sang at first hesitantly, but seizing the song quickly, made up for hesitation by added gusto in the response. Always the strong voice of the leader corrected errors until the song was perfectly learned. "Singing" Johnson must have derived his support in somewhat the same way as the preachers,—part of a collection, food and lodging. He doubtless spent his leisure time in originating new words and melodies and new lines for old songs. "Singing" Johnson is one of the indelible pictures on my mind. A small but stocky, dark-brown man was he, with one eye, and possessing a clear, strong, high-pitched voice. Not as striking a figure as some of the great Negro preachers I used to see and hear, but at camp meetings, revivals, and on special occasions only slightly less important than any of them. A maker of songs and a wonderful leader of singing. A man who could improvise lines on the moment. A great judge of the appropriate song to sing; and with a delicate sense of when to come to the preacher's support after a climax in the sermon had been reached by breaking in with a line or two of a song that expressed a certain sentiment, often just a single line. "Singing" Johnson always sang with his eyes, or eye, closed, and indicated the tempo by swinging his head and body. When he warmed to his work it was easy to see that he was transported and utterly oblivious to his surroundings.

"Singing" Johnson was of the line of the mightier bards of an earlier day, and he exemplified how they worked and how the Spirituals were "composed." These bards, I believe, made the original inventions of story and song, which in turn were influenced or modified by the group in action.

In form the Spirituals often run strictly parallel with African songs, incremental leading lines and choral iteration. Krehbiel quotes from Denham and Clapperton's *Narrative of Travels in Northern and Central Africa,* the following song by Negro bards of Bornou in praise of their Sultan:

> Give flesh to the hyenas at daybreak—
> Oh, the broad spears!
> The spear of the Sultan is the broadest—
> Oh, the broad spears!

PREFACE

I behold thee now, I desire to see none other—
  Oh, the broad spears!
My horse is as tall as a high wall—
  Oh, the broad spears!
He will fight ten—he fears nothing!
  Oh, the broad spears!
He has slain ten, the guns are yet behind—
  Oh, the broad spears!
The elephant of the forest brings me what I want—
  Oh, the broad spears!
Like unto thee, so is the Sultan—
  Oh, the broad spears!
Be brave! Be brave, my friends and kinsmen—
  Oh, the broad spears!
God is great! I wax fierce as a beast of prey—
  Oh, the broad spears!
God is great! Today those I wished for are come—
  Oh, the broad spears!

Or take this beautiful song found in one of the Bantu folk-tales. It is the song of an old woman standing at the edge of the river with a babe in her arms, singing to coax back the child's mother, who has been enchanted and taken by the river. The tale is *The Story of Tangalimlibo,* and the song runs as follows:

It is crying, it is crying,
  Sihamba Ngenyanga.
The child of the walker by moonlight,
  Sihamba Ngenyanga.
It was done intentionally by people, whose names cannot be mentioned
  Sihamba Ngenyanga.
They sent her for water during the day,
  Sihamba Ngenyanga.
She tried to dip it with the milk basket, and then it sank,
  Sihamba Ngenyanga.
Tried to dip it with the ladle, and then it sank,
  Sihamba Ngenyanga.
Tried to dip it with the mantle, and then it sank,
  Sihamba Ngenyanga.

24

PREFACE

Compare these African songs with the American Spiritual, *Oh, Wasn't Dat a Wide Ribber*:

> Oh, de Ribber of Jordan is deep and wide,
>   One mo' ribber to cross.
> I don't know how to get on de other side,
>   One mo' ribber to cross.
> Oh, you got Jesus, hold him fast,
>   One mo' ribber to cross.
> Oh, better love was nebber told,
>   One mo' ribber to cross.
> 'Tis stronger dan an iron band,
>   One mo' ribber to cross.
> 'Tis sweeter dan de honey comb,
>   One mo' ribber to cross.
> Oh, de good ole chariot passin' by,
>   One mo' ribber to cross.
> She jarred de earth an' shook de sky,
>   One mo' ribber to cross.
> I pray, good Lord, I shall be one,
>   One mo' ribber to cross.
> To get in de chariot an' trabble on,
>   One mo' ribber to cross.
> We're told dat de fore wheel run by love,
>   One mo' ribber to cross.
> We're told dat de hind wheel run by faith,
>   One mo' ribber to cross.
> I hope I'll get dere by an' bye,
>   One mo' ribber to cross.
> To jine de number in de sky,
>   One mo' ribber to cross.
> Oh, Jordan's Ribber am chilly an' cold,
>   One mo' ribber to cross.
> It chills de body, but not de soul,
>   One mo' ribber to cross.

A study of the Spirituals leads to the belief that the earlier ones were built upon the form so common to African songs, leading lines and response. It would be safe, I think, to say that the bulk of the Spirituals

25

are cast in this simple form. Among those following this simple structure, however, are some of the most beautiful of the slave songs. One of these, whose beauty is unsurpassed, is *Swing Low, Sweet Chariot*, which is constructed to be sung in the following manner:

Leader:	Swing low, sweet chariot,
Congregation:	Comin' for to carry me home.
Leader:	Swing low, sweet chariot,
Congregation:	Comin' for to carry me home.
Leader:	I look over Jordan, what do I see?
Congregation:	Comin' for to carry me home.
Leader:	A band of angels comin' after me,
Congregation:	Comin' for to carry me home.
Leader:	Swing low, sweet chariot,
	etc., etc., etc.

The solitary voice of the leader is answered by a sound like a rolling sea. The effect produced is strangely moving.

But as the American Negro went a step beyond his original African music in the development of melody and harmony, he also went a step beyond in the development of form. The lead and response are still retained, but the response is developed into a true chorus. In a number of the songs there are leads, a response and a chorus. In this class of songs the chorus becomes the most important part, dominating the whole song and coming first. Such a song is the well known "Steal Away to Jesus." In this song the congregation begins with the chorus, singing it in part harmony:

> Steal away, steal away,
> Steal away to Jesus.
> Steal away, steal away home,
> I ain't got long to stay here.

Then the leader alone or the congregation in unison:

> My Lord He calls me,
> He calls me by the thunder,
> The trumpet sounds within-a my soul.

Then the response in part harmony:

> I ain't got long to stay here.

> Steal away, steal away,
>   etc., etc., etc.

This developed form is carried a degree farther in "Go Down Moses." Here the congregation opens with the powerful theme of the chorus, singing it in unison down to the last line, which is harmonized:

> Go down, Moses,
> 'Way down in Egypt land,
> Tell ole Pharaoh,
> Let my people go.

Then the leader:

> Thus saith the Lord, bold Moses said,

And the response:

> Let my people go.

Leader:

> If not I'll smite your first-born dead.

Response:

> Let my people go.

Chorus:

> Go down, Moses,
> Go down, Moses,
> 'Way down in Egypt land,
> Tell ole Pharaoh,
> Let my people go.
>   etc., etc., etc.

In a few of the songs this development is carried to a point where the form becomes almost purely choral. Examples of these more complex structures are, *Deep River,* and *Walk Together Children.*

27

PREFACE

I have said that the European concept of music, generally speaking, is melody and the African concept is rhythm. It is upon this point that most white people have difficulty with Negro music, the difficulty of getting the "swing" of it. White America has pretty well mastered this difficulty; and naturally, because the Negro has been beating these rhythms in its ears for three hundred years. But in Europe, in spite of the vogue of American popular music, based on these rhythms, the best bands are not able to play it satisfactorily. Of course, they play the notes correctly, but any American can at once detect that there is something lacking. The trouble is, they play the notes too correctly; and do not play what is not written down. There are few things more ludicrous—to an American—than the efforts of a European music hall artist to sing a jazz song. It is interesting, if not curious, that among white Americans those who have mastered these rhythms most completely are Jewish-Americans. Indeed, Jewish musicians and composers are they who have carried them to their highest development in written form.

In all authentic American Negro music the rhythms may be divided roughly into two classes—rhythms based on the swinging of head and body and rhythms based on the patting of hands and feet. Again, speaking roughly, the rhythms of the Spirituals fall in the first class and the rhythms of secular music in the second class. The "swing" of the Spirituals is an altogether subtle and elusive thing. It is subtle and elusive because it is in perfect union with the religious ecstasy that manifests itself in the swaying bodies of a whole congregation, swaying as if responding to the baton of some extremely sensitive conductor. So it is very difficult, if not impossible, to sing these songs sitting or standing coldly still, and at the same time capture the spontaneous "swing" which is of their very essence.

Carl Van Vechten writing in *Vanity Fair* about these songs declared it as his opinion that white singers cannot sing them, and that women, with few exceptions, should not attempt to sing them at all. Mr. Van Vechten made this statement in recognition of the element in the Spirituals without which their beauty of melody and harmony is lifeless. His statement also, I take it, has specific reference to the singing of these songs as solos on the concert stage. I agree that white

28

singers are, naturally, prone to go to either of two extremes: to attempt to render a Spiritual as though it were a Brahms song, or to assume a "Negro unctuousness" that is obviously false, and painfully so. I think white singers, concert singers, *can* sing Spirituals— if they *feel* them. But to feel them it is necessary to know the truth about their origin and history, to get in touch with the association of ideas that surround them, and to realize something of what they have meant in the experiences of the people who created them. In a word, the capacity to *feel* these songs while singing them is more important than any amount of mere artistic technique. Singers who take the Spirituals as mere "art" songs and singers who make of them an exhibition of what is merely amusing or exotic are equally doomed to failure, so far as true interpretation is concerned. Mr. Van Vechten's opinion brings up the question of the rendition of these songs as concert solos not only by white but by colored singers. I have seen more than one colored singer floundering either in the "art" or the "exhibition" pit. The truth is, these songs, primarily created and constructed, as they were, for group singing, will always remain a high test for the individual artist. They are not concert material for the mediocre soloist. Through the genius and supreme artistry of Roland Hayes these songs undergo, we may say, a transfiguration. He takes them high above the earth and sheds over them shimmering silver of moonlight and flashes of the sun's gold; and we are transported as he sings. By a seemingly opposite method, through sheer simplicity, without any conscious attempt at artistic effort and by devoted adherence to the primitive traditions, Paul Robeson achieves substantially the same effect. These two singers, apparently so different, have the chief essential in common; they both feel the Spirituals deeply. Mr. Hayes, notwithstanding all his artistry, sings these songs with tears on his cheeks. Both these singers pull at the heart strings and moisten the eyes of their listeners.

We were discussing the "swing" of the Spirituals, and were saying how subtle and elusive a thing it was. It is the more subtle and elusive because there is a still further intricacy in the rhythms. The swaying of the body marks the regular beat or, better, surge, for it is something stronger than a beat, and is more or less, not precisely,

29

strict in time; but the Negro loves nothing better in his music than to play with the fundamental time beat. He will, as it were, take the fundamental beat and pound it out with his left hand, almost monotonously; while with his right hand he juggles it. It should be noted that even in the swaying of head and body the head marks the surge off in shorter waves than does the body. In listening to Negroes sing their own music it is often tantalizing and even exciting to watch a minute fraction of a beat balancing for a slight instant on the bar between two measures, and, when it seems almost too late, drop back into its own proper compartment. There is a close similarity between this singing and the beating of the big drum and the little drums by the African natives. In addition, there are the curious turns and twists and quavers and the intentional striking of certain notes just a shade off the key, with which the Negro loves to embellish his songs. These tendencies constitute a handicap that has baffled many of the recorders of this music. I doubt that it is possible with our present system of notation to make a fixed transcription of these peculiarities that would be absolutely true; for in their very nature they are not susceptible to fixation. Many of the transcriptions that have been made are far from the true manner and spirit of singing the Spirituals. I have gone thus far into the difficulties connected with singing the Spirituals in order that those who are interested in these songs may have a fuller understanding of just what they are. It is not necessary to say that the lack of complete mastery of all these difficulties is not at all fatal to deriving pleasure from singing Spirituals. A group does not have to be able to sing with the fervor and abandon of a Negro congregation to enjoy them. Nor does one have to be a Hayes or a Robeson to give others an idea of their beauty and power.

Going back again, the rhythms of Negro secular music, roughly speaking, fall in the class based on the patting of hands and feet. It can easily be seen that this distinction between the Spirituals and Negro secular music is, in a large way, that of different physical responses to differing sets of emotions. Religious ecstasy fittingly manifests itself in swaying heads and bodies; the emotions that call for hand and foot patting are pleasure, humor, hilarity, love, just the joy of being alive. In this class of his music, as in the Spirituals, the Negro is true to the characteristic of playing with the fundamental beat; if anything, more so. What is largely psychological manifestation in the Spirituals becomes physical response in the secular music. In this music the fundamental beat is chiefly maintained by the patting of one foot, while the hands clap out intricate and varying rhythmic patterns. It should be understood that the foot is not marking straight time, but what Negroes call "stop time," or what the books have no better definition for than "syncopation." The strong accent or down beat is never lost, but is playfully bandied from hand to foot and from foot to hand.

I wish to point out here that the rhapsodical hand clapping connected with singing the Spirituals—except in the "ring shout" songs, of which I shall speak later—is not to be confused with the hand clapping to dance-time music. Recently another Negro dance has swept the country. It was introduced to New York by Messrs. Miller and Lyles in their musical comedy, *Runnin' Wild*. And at present white people everywhere, in the cabarets, on the ball floor and at home count it an accomplishment to be able to "do the Charleston." When Miller and Lyles introduced the dance in their play they did not depend wholly on the orchestra—an extraordinary jazz band—for the accompaniment, but had the major part of the chorus supplement it with hand and foot patting. The effect was electrical and contagious. It was the best demonstration of beating out complex rhythms I have ever witnessed; and, I do not believe New York ever before witnessed anything of just its sort.

It would be interesting to know how many peoples there are other than the Negro in America and Africa, if there are any, who innately beat out these complex and extremely intricate rhythms with their hands and feet. The Spanish people do something of the kind in their castanet dances; but, as has already been shown, this is probably the result of African influence. At any rate, this innate characteristic of the Negro in America is the genesis and foundation of our national popular medium for musical expression.

The temptations for these digressions are almost irresistible. At this point the writer could go far along the line of discussing the origin of Negro secular music and its development until it was finally

31

taken over and made "American popular music." It would be easy also to stray along a parallel line, and note how Negro dances have kept step with Negro secular music, and how from their inglorious beginnings they have advanced until they have been recognized and accepted by the stage and by "society." And this merely to pave the way for another slight digression. And, yet, we can hardly discuss the question of Negro rhythms and "swing" without paying some attention to still another class of songs—the work songs.

With regard to rhythm and "swing" the work songs do not fall into the classification with either the Spirituals or the dance-time songs. The "swing" of these songs is governed by the rhythmic motions made by a gang of men at labor. It may be the motions made in swinging a pick on the road or a hammer on the rock pile, or in loading cotton on the levée. Some of the finest examples of these songs are those originated by the convicts at work in the chain gang. One of these is the poignantly beautiful "Water Boy" frequently sung by Roland Hayes. All the men sing and move together as they swing their picks or rock-breaking hammers. They move like a ballet; not a ballet of cavorting legs and pirouetting feet, but a ballet of bending backs and quivering muscles. It is all in rhythm but a rhythm impossible to set down. There is always a leader and he sets the pace. A phrase is sung while the shining hammers are being lifted. It is cut off suddenly as the hammers begin to descend and gives place to a prolonged grunt which becomes explosive at the impact of the blow. Each phrase of the song is independent, apparently obeying no law of time. After each impact the hammers lie still and there is silence. As they begin to rise again the next phrase of the song is sung; and so on. Just how long the hammers will be allowed to rest cannot be determined; nor, since the movements are not governed by strict time, can any exact explanation be given as to why they all begin to rise simultaneously. There are variations that violate the obvious laws of rhythm, but over it all can be discerned a superior rhythmic law. A fine illustration of what I have been trying to explain was given by Paul Robeson in his rendition of the convict song in "The Emperor Jones."

Brief mention must be made of another class of Negro songs. This

32

is a remnant of songs allied to the Spirituals but which cannot be strictly classified with them. They are the "shout songs." These songs are not true spirituals nor even truly religious; in fact, they are not actually songs. They might be termed quasi-religious or semi-barbaric music. They once were used, and still are in a far less degree, in religious gatherings, but neither musically nor in the manner of their use do they fall in the category of the Spirituals. This term "shout songs" has no reference to the loud, jubilant Spirituals, which are often so termed by writers on Negro music; it has reference to the songs or, better, the chants used to accompany the "ring shout." The "ring shout," in truth, is nothing more or less than the survival of a primitive African dance, which in quite an understandable way attached itself in the early days to the Negro's Christian worship. I can remember seeing this dance many times when I was a boy. A space is cleared by moving the benches, and the men and women arrange themselves, generally alternately, in a ring, their bodies quite close. The music starts and the ring begins to move. Around it goes, at first slowly, then with quickening pace. Around and around it moves on shuffling feet that do not leave the floor, one foot beating with the heel a decided accent in strict two-four time. The music is supplemented by the clapping of hands. As the ring goes around it begins to take on signs of frenzy. The music, starting, perhaps, with a Spiritual, becomes a wild, monotonous chant. The same musical phrase is repeated over and over one, two, three, four, five hours. The words become a repetition of an incoherent cry. The very monotony of sound and motion produces an ecstatic state. Women, screaming, fall to the ground prone and quivering. Men, exhausted, drop out of the shout. But the ring closes up and moves around and around.

I remember, too, that even then the "ring shout" was looked upon as a very questionable form of worship. It was distinctly frowned upon by a great many colored people. Indeed, I do not recall ever seeing a "ring shout" except *after* the regular services. Almost whispered invitations would go around, "Stay after church; there's going to be a 'ring shout.'" The more educated ministers and members, as fast as they were able to brave the primitive element in the churches, placed a ban on the "ring shout." The "shout," however, was never universal. The best information that I have been able to gather indicates that it was most general in the Atlantic and Gulf coastal regions of the south-eastern states. Today it is rarely seen. It has not quite, but has almost disappeared. In parts of Louisiana, and in some parts of the West Indies and South America, or, in other words, where the Negro came under the influence and jurisdiction of the Catholic Church and the Church of England this dance long persisted outside of the church and Christian religion. There it retained its primitive social and ceremonial significance and was practiced with more or less frankness. Two reasons may be advanced to cover these two facts: under the Catholic Church and the Church of England the Negro, practically, never had any place of worship of his own, and, of course, he would never have been allowed to introduce such a practice as the "ring shout," even under a religious guise, into those churches; it is also in a large measure true that the Negro in those localities has never accepted the Christian religion in the sense and degree in which it was accepted by the Negro of the South; there his acceptance was more a matter of outward conformity, and he clung more tenaciously to his African cultural and religious ideas. This survival of an African ceremony has been outlawed in the United States and cannot be seen except in some backward churches of a backward community. But in parts of the West Indies and South America it is still quite frankly practiced as a social function. The Negroes that live along the eastern fringe of Venezuela dance every Saturday. I have often heard their chants and the drums throbbing until far into the night. I was in Haiti several years ago and I learned that the "Saturday night dance," which had been the custom there, too, had been interdicted in the larger cities by the American Occupation authorities. However, the people were still allowed to dance in the rural districts and on holidays. On one national holiday in a small village I saw them dance under a thatched pavilion in the little public square. It was the same thing I had seen in my childhood in a small church in Florida. The formation of the dancers was the same, the shuffling motion was the same, the monotonous, incoherent chant sounded the same, although these folk spoke an unfamiliar language. The only differences I noted were: it was not in a church,

34

there was great gaiety instead of religious frenzy, and the beating drums—real African drums.

I refer again to Mr. Van Vechten's interesting article. In it he said, "Negro folksongs differ from the folksongs of most other races through the fact that they are sung in harmony." I am glad to have this confirmation of my own opinion. I have long thought that the harmonization of the Spirituals by the folk group in singing them was distinctive of them among the folksongs of the world. My speculation was with regard to how many other groups of folksongs there were that were harmonized spontaneously in the singing. The fact that the Spirituals were sung in harmony has always seemed natural to me, because Negroes harmonize instinctively. What about the traditional reputation of Negroes as singers; upon what is it really founded? The common idea is that it is founded upon the quality of their voices. It is not. The voices of Negroes, when untrained, are often overloud, perhaps rather blatant, sometimes even a bit strident; but they are *never discordant*. In harmony they take on an orchestra-like timbre. The popular credit given to Negroes as singers is given, maybe unconsciously, because of their ability to harmonize, and not because of the quality of their voices. When the folks at the "big house" sat on the verandah and heard the singing floating up through the summer night from the "quarters" they were enchanted; and it is likely they did not realize that the enchantment was wrought chiefly through the effect produced by harmonizing and not by the voices as voices.

Pick up four colored boys or young men anywhere and the chances are ninety out of a hundred that you have a quartet. Let one of them sing the melody and the others will naturally find the parts. Indeed, it may be said that all male Negro youth of the United States is divided into quartets. When I was a very small boy one of my greatest pleasures was going to concerts and hearing the crack quartets made up of waiters in the Jacksonville hotels sing. Each of the big Florida resort hotels boasted at least two quartets, a first and a second. When I was fifteen and my brother was thirteen we were singing in a quartet which competed with other quartets. In the days when such a thing as a white barber was unknown in the South, every barber shop had its quartet, and the men spent their leisure time playing on the guitar —not banjo, mind you—and "harmonizing." I have witnessed some of these explorations in the field of harmony and the scenes of hilarity and back-slapping when a new and peculiarly rich chord was discovered. There would be demands for repetitions, and cries of "Hold it! Hold it!" until it was firmly mastered. And well it was, for some of these chords were so new and strange for voices that, like Sullivan's *Lost Chord*, they would never have been found again except for the celerity with which they were recaptured. In this way was born the famous but much abused "barber-shop chord."

It may sound like an extravagant claim, but it is, nevertheless a fact that the "barber-shop chord" is the foundation of the close harmony method adopted by American musicians in making arrangements for male voices. I do not think English musicians have yet used this method of arranging to any great extent. "Barber-shop harmonies" gave a tremendous vogue to male quartet singing, first on the minstrel stage, then in vaudeville; and soon white young men, wherever four or more were gathered together, tried themselves at "harmonizing." The vogue somewhat declined because the old "barber-shop chord" was so overdone that it became almost taboo. But the male quartet is still one of the main features of colored musical shows. These modern quartets avoid the stereotyped chords of twenty, thirty and forty years ago, but the chief charm of their singing still lies in the closeness of the harmony. No one who heard *Shuffle Along,* can forget the singing of *The Four Harmony Kings.*

Among the early collectors of the Spirituals there was some doubt as to whether they were sung in harmony. This confusion may have been due in part to the fact that in the Spirituals the Negro makes such frequent use of unison harmony. The leading lines are always sung by a single voice or in unison harmony, and many of the refrains or choruses are sung in unison harmony down to the last phrase, and then in part harmony. The chorus of *Go Down Moses* is an example. In *Slave Songs of the United States,* published in 1867, Mr. Allen, one of the editors, in accounting for the fact that only the melodies of the songs in the collection were printed, said in his preface:

36

PREFACE

"There is no singing in parts, as we understand it, and yet no two seem to be singing the same thing; the leading singer starts the words of each verse, often improvising, and others, who 'base' him, as it is called, strike in with the refrain or even join in the solo when the words are familiar. When the 'base' begins the leader often stops, leaving the rest of the words to be guessed at, or it may be they are taken up by one of the other singers. And the 'basers' themselves seem to follow their own whims, beginning where they please, striking an octave above or below (in case they have pitched the tune too high), or hitting some other note that chords, so as to produce the effect of a marvelous complication and variety and yet with the most perfect time and rarely with any discord. And what makes it all the harder to unravel a thread of melody out of this strange network is that, like birds, they seem not infrequently to strike sounds that cannot be precisely represented by the gamut and abound in 'slides' from one note to another and turns and cadences not in articulated notes."

Mr. Allen's opinion that the songs were not harmonized is explained when he says, "There is no singing in parts, as we understand it." And no one can blame him for not attempting to do more than transcribe the melodies. If Mr. Allen were writing today, when America is so familiar with the bizarre Negro harmonies, he would recognize that the Spirituals were harmonized and he would try to transcribe the harmonies. What he heard was the primitive and spontaneous group singing of the Spirituals, and his description of it is, perhaps, as good as can be given. It might also be noted that it is an excellent description of the most modern American form of instrumentation, —a form that most people think of as a brand new invention.

The songs collected in this book have been arranged for solo voice, but in the piano accompaniments the arrangers have sincerely striven to give the characteristic harmonies that would be used in spontaneous group singing. Of course, these harmonies are not fixed. A group or congregation singing spontaneously might never use precisely the same harmonies twice; however, Mr. Rosamond Johnson and Mr. Brown have shown great fidelity to what is characteristic. The ordinary four-part harmonies can, without difficulty, be picked out from the accompaniments to most of the songs, but what the arrangers

37

had principally in mind was to have the instrumentation approach the effect of the singing group in action.

What can be said about the poetry of the texts of the Spirituals? Naturally, not so much as can be said about the music. In the use of the English language both the bards and the group worked under limitations that might appear to be hopeless. Many of the lines are less than trite, and irrelevant repetition often becomes tiresome. They are often saved alone by their naïveté. And yet there is poetry, and a surprising deal of it in the Spirituals. There is more than ought to be reasonably expected from a forcedly ignorant people working in an absolutely alien language. Hebraic paraphrases are frequent. These are accounted for by the fact that the Bible was the chief source of material for the lines of these songs.

> Upon de mountain Jehovah spoke,
> Out-a his mouth came fi-ar and smoke.

But in these paraphrases we have something that is not exactly paraphrase; there is a change of, I dare to say it, style; something Hebrew—austerity—is lessened, and something Negro—charm—is injected. Examples could be multiplied:

> I wrastled wid Satan, I wrastled wid sin
> Stepped over hell, an' come back agin.

> Isaiah mounted on de wheel of time
> Spoke to God A-mighty 'way down de line.

> O hear dat lumberin' thunder
> A-roll f'om door to door,
> A-callin' de people home to God,
> Dey'll git home bime-by.

> O see dat forkéd lightenin'
> A-jump f'om cloud to cloud,
> A-pickin' up God's chillun
> Dey'll git home bime-by.

Here are lines suggestive of what may be found in the Psalms; and yet how distinctively different:

PREFACE

Sinner, sinner, you better pray,
Looks like my Lord a-comin' in de sky.
Or yo' soul be los' on de jedgment day,
Looks like my Lord a-comin' in de sky.

O little did I think he was so nigh,
Looks like my Lord a-comin' in de sky.
He spoke an' he made me laugh and cry,
Looks like my Lord a-comin' in de sky.

When I was a monah jes like you,
Looks like my Lord a-comin' in de sky.
My head got wet wid de midnight dew,
Looks like my Lord a-comin' in de sky.

My head got wet wid de midnight dew,
Looks like my Lord a-comin' in de sky.
De mornin' star was a witness too,
Looks like my Lord a-comin' in de sky.

Many of the stories and scenes in the Bible gave the Negro bards
great play for their powers of graphic description. The stories are
always dramatic and the pictures vivid and gorgeously colored. The
style, in contradiction of the general idea of Negro diffuseness, is
concise and condensed. It might be said of them that every line is
a picture. The following illustrative lines are taken from a Spiritual
derived from John's vision on Patmos:

Yes, the book of Revelations will be brought forth dat day,
An' ev'ry leaf unfolded, the book of the seven seals.

An' I went down to Egypt, I camped upon de groun'
At de soundin' of de trumpet de Holy Ghost came down.

An' when de seals were opened, the voice said, ''Come an' see,''
I went an' stood a-lookin to see de mystery.

The red horse came a-gallopin', an' de black horse he came too,
An' de pale horse he came down de road, an' stole my father away.

An' den I see ole Satan, an' dey bound him wid a chain,
An' dey put him in de fi-ar, an' I see de smoke arise.

39

PREFACE

Dey bound him in de fi-ar, where he wanted to take my soul,
Ole Satan gnashed his teeth and howled, he missed po' sinner man's soul.

Den I see de dead arisin', an' stan' before de Lamb
An' de wicked call on de mountains to hide dem f'om His face.

An' den I see de Christians standin' on God's right hand,
A shoutin' "Hallelujah!" singing praises to de Lamb.

Sometimes these biblical incidents are resolved into lyrical gems. I quote a stanza from the song about Jacob wrestling with the angel, found in Colonel Thomas Wentworth Higginson's book:

O wrestlin' Jacob, Jacob day's a-breakin',
I will not let thee go!
O wrestlin' Jacob, Jacob day's a-breakin',
He will not let me go!
O, I hold my brudder wid a tremblin' hand;
I would not let him go!
I hold my sister wid a tremblin' hand;
I would not let her go!

But see what these Negro bards have done with the story of the crucifixion. They have not merely rehearsed it as it is given in the gospels: they have fused into it their very own pathos:

Dey crucified my Lord,
An' He never said a mumblin' word.
Dey crucified my Lord,
An' he never said a mumblin' word,
Not a word—not a word—not a word.

Dey nailed Him to de tree,
An' He never said a mumblin' word.
Dey nailed Him to de tree,
An' He never said a mumblin' word,
Not a word—not a word—not a word.

Dey pierced Him in de side,
An' He never said a mumblin' word.
Dey pierced Him in de side,

40

PREFACE

> An' He never said a mumblin' word,
> Not a word—not a word—not a word.
>
> De blood came twinklin' down,
>   An' He never said a mumblin' word.
> De blood came twinklin' down,
>   An' He never said a mumblin' word,
> Not a word—not a word—not a word.
>
> He bowed His head an' died,
>   An' He never said a mumblin' word.
> He bowed His head and died,
>   An' He never said a mumblin' word,
> Not a word—not a word—not a word.

The word "twinklin'" in the fourth stanza is a Negro pronunciation of the word "trinkling." But in this way what a magical poetic phrase was stumbled upon, "The blood came twinkling down."

In rare instances a touch of the irrepressible Negro humor creeps in:

> Ev'ybody talkin' 'bout heaben ain' gwine der.
>
> Sister, you better mind how you walk on de cross,
> Yo' foot might slip an' yo' soul git los'.
>
> De devil is a liar an' a conjurer too,
> Ef you don't look out he'll conjure you.

Much, too, of the poetry of the Spirituals is the Negro's innate expression of his own emotions and experiences; and out of these he drew some piercing lyrical cries:

> Sometimes I feel like a motherless child,
> Sometimes I feel like a motherless child,
> Sometimes I feel like a motherless child,
> A long ways from home.

Or in the opposite mood:

> Sometimes I feel like an eagle in de air
> Some-a dese mornin's bright an' fair
> I'm goin' to lay down my heavy load;
> Goin' to spread my wings an' cleave de air.

41

PREFACE

You may bury me in de east,
You may bury me in de west,
But I'll hear de trumpet sound
In-a dat mornin'.

Occasionally we are startled by a flash of poetry of pure beauty; of poetry not circumscribed by individual conditions, but coming out of the experiences of humanity. I quote, in concluding these examples, again from Colonel Higginson's book:

I know moon-rise, I know star-rise,
  I lay dis body down.
I walk in de moonlight, I walk in de starlight,
  To lay dis body down.
I walk in de graveyard, I walk throo de graveyard,
  To lay dis body down.
I lie in de grave an' stretch out my arms,
  I lay dis body down.
I go to de jedgment in de evenin' of de day
  When I lay dis body down,
An' my soul an' your soul will meet in de day
  When I lay dis body down.

Regarding the line, "I lie in de grave an' stretch out my arms," Colonel Higginson wrote: "Never, it seems to me, since man first lived and suffered, was his infinite longing for peace uttered more plaintively than in that line."

Something should be said to give a general idea about the "language" in which these songs were written. Negro dialect in America is the result of the effort of the slave to establish a medium of communication between himself and his master. This he did by dropping his original language, and formulating a phonologically and grammatically simplified English; that is, an English in which the harsh and difficult sounds were elided, and the secondary moods and tenses were eliminated. This dialect served not only as a means of communication between slave and master but also between slave and slave; so the original African languages became absolutely lost. The dialect spoken in the sea islands off the coast of Georgia and South Carolina remains

42

closer to African form than the dialect of any other section, and still contains some African words. It is, at any rate, farther from English than the speech of American Negroes anywhere else. But it is remarkable how few words of known African origin there are in the Negro dialect generally spoken throughout the United States.

Negro dialect, in substantially its present form, has been used in the United States for the past two centuries. In the South all white people, men, women and children, understand the dialect without any shadow of difficulty. Indeed, the English spoken by the whites does not differ, in some respects, from the dialect; so great has been the influence of this soft, indolent speech of the Negro. Nevertheless, Negro dialect presents some difficulties to white people who have never lived in the South, when they attempt to reproduce it in speech or in song. Of course, it is not necessary to be an expert in Negro dialect to sing the Spirituals, but most of them lose in charm when they are sung in straight English. For example, it would be next to sacrilege to render:

"What kinda shoes you gwine to weah?"

by:

"What kind of shoes are you going to wear?"

An error that confuses many persons is the idea that Negro dialect is uniform and fixed. The idioms and pronunciation of the dialect vary in different sections of the South. A Negro of the uplands of Georgia does not speak the identical dialect of his brother of the islands off the coast of the state, and would have a hard time understanding him. Nor is the generally spoken Negro dialect the fixed thing it is made to be on the printed page. It is variable and fluid. Not even in the dialect of any particular section is a given word always pronounced the same. It may vary slightly in the next breath in the mouth of the same speaker. How a word is pronounced is governed by the preceding and following sounds. Sometimes the combination permits of a liaison so close that to the uninitiated the sound of the word is almost lost.

To illustrate: If one dialect-speaking Negro asks another, "Is dat all you got to say?" the answer in the affirmative would be "Das all."

PREFACE

The invariable practice on the printed page is to represent "that" by "dat" and, logically, "that's" by "dat's." But the harsh "ts" sound is displeasing to the Negro ear, as well as troublesome to the Negro tongue, so it is softened into "das."

Negro dialect is for many people made unintelligible on the printed page by the absurd practice of devising a clumsy, outlandish, so-called phonetic spelling for words in a dialect story or poem when the regular English spelling represents the very same sound. Paul Laurence Dunbar did a great deal to reform the writing down of dialect, but since it is more a matter of ear than of rules those who are not intimately familiar with the sounds continue to make the same blunders.

Since the understanding of the Spirituals and the pleasure of singing them are increased by a knowledge of the dialect in which the texts were composed, a suggestion or two about it will not be out of place. The first thing to remember is that the dialect is fundamentally English. An American from any part of the United States or an Englishman can, with not more than slight difficulty, understand it when it is spoken. The trouble comes in trying to get it from the printed page. There are some idioms that may be strange, but they are few. The next thing to remember is that the pronunciation of the dialect is the result of the elision by the Negro, as far as possible, of all troublesome consonants and sound combinations.

Thus: "th" as in "that" or "than" becomes "d"
"th" as in "thick" or "thin" becomes "t"

This rule holds good at the end as well as at the beginning of words and syllables. So we have "dat" and "der" or "dar," and "tick" and "tin," and "wid" and "det" (for death). Indeed, the Negro tries to elide the "h" whenever it is in combination with another consonant. There is always the tendency to suppress the "r," except when it is the initial letter of the syllable. The "g" in "ing" endings is generally dropped or smothered, and the sound resembles the final French "m" and "n." "A," "e" and "u," between two consonants in an unaccented syllable, are uniformly rendered by the sound of "u" in "but." The sound is sometimes broadened almost to the "a" in

44

"father." This is not an inflexible rule, but it especially holds true with regard to final syllables. (It may be remembered that this same tendency, in a less degree, is true of correct English.) Examples: The word "never" may be heard either as "nevuh" or as "nevah." This word is often playfully emphasized by a strong accent on the last syllable, "neváh." In the word "better" the first "e" has the usual short "e" sound, and the second "e" follows the above rule. Thus we have "bettuh" or "bettah." The word "to" is always pronounced "tuh." The "or" and "our" combinations are generally sounded "oh," as "do'" or "doh" for "door," and "monuh" or "monah" for "mourner." This dialect word, by the way, does not signify one undergoing grief, but one undergoing repentance for sins.

Perhaps the most common mistake made in imitating Negro dialect is in giving to "de," the dialect for "the," the unvarying pronunciation of "dee." It is pronounced "dee" when it precedes words beginning with a vowel sound, and "duh" before those beginning with a consonant sound. In this it follows the rule for the article "the."

The statement that the Negro dialect generally spoken in the United States is fundamentally English brings up a curious fact regarding the effort of a smaller group of Negro slaves to create a medium of communication between themselves and their masters. This fact is the more apropos because this smaller group also created a rich body of folksongs. In what was the Territory of Louisiana the language was French. The Negro slaves of the Territory, in establishing a medium of communication, instead of forming a dialect of the French language, created a distinct language. This language is known as Creole. Creole is an Africanized French, but it is neither African nor French. It is a language in itself. The French-speaking person cannot, with the exception of some words, understand it unless he learns it. Creole is a distinct language, scientifically constructed and logical in its grammatical arrangement. It is a graphic and expressive language, and is, in some respects, superior to French.

For a reason I cannot give, wherever there was a Negro population the French language in the French-American colonial settlements divided itself into two branches—French and Creole. This is true of Louisiana, of Martinique, of Guadaloupe and of Haiti. No such thing happened with the Spanish language. Negroes in the Spanish-American countries speak Spanish.

In setting down the words of the songs here included I have endeavored to keep them as true to the original dialect as is compatible with a more or less ready recognition of what the words really are. When a dialect spelling would puzzle and confuse the reader and actually throw him off, the regular English spelling has been followed. This, for example, was the practice followed in writing the word "sword" in the song *Singing With a Sword in My Hand*. The spelling "sode" or "soad" would have been positively misleading. I am sure this method is preferable to an attempt to indicate by phonetic spelling all the exact sounds of Negro dialect. I have seen "unuthuh" printed for "another." The ordinary pronunciation of the regular English spelling is so close to the dialect that the difference does not warrant such a task in deciphering being placed upon the reader. It will be noticed that in some of the songs the exaggerated form of dialect would not be fitting; in such songs I have kept the dialect forms down to the minimum. With a general idea of the principles of the dialect the reader or singer may give even Negro songs written in straight English the proper color.

This book is dedicated to those through whose efforts these songs have been collected, preserved and given to the world. It is a fitting, if inadequate, tribute; for it was wholly within the possibilities for these songs to be virtually lost. The people who created them were not capable of recording them, and the conditions out of which this music sprang and by which it was nourished have almost passed away. Without the direct effort on the part of those to whom I offer this slight tribute, the Spirituals would probably have fallen into disuse and finally disappeared. This probability is increased by the fact that they passed through a period following Emancipation when the front ranks of the colored people themselves would have been willing and even glad to let them die.

The first efforts towards the preservation of this music were made by the pioneer collectors who worked within the decade following the Civil War. These collectors, either through curiosity or as a matter

46

of research, or because they were impressed by the unique beauty of the Spirituals, set down on paper the words and melodies. All of them were more or less successful in getting the melodies down correctly, but none of these pioneers even attempted to set down the anarchic harmonies which they heard. In fact, they had no classification for these sounds or even comprehension of them as harmonies. These pioneers were none of them exceptionally trained, but on this point they were not one whit behind the most advanced thought in American music of their day. Some of these early collectors contented themselves with jotting down simply the melodies and words, and publishing their collections in that form. Others harmonized the melodies. These harmonized arrangements, however, had little or no relation to the original harmonies or the manner of singing them by the group. They were, generally, straight four-part arrangements set down in strict accordance with the standard rules of thorough-bass. Nevertheless, except for the work of these pioneer collectors, done mostly as a labor of love, the number of the Spirituals recorded and preserved would have been only a small fraction of what it is.

The credit for the first introduction of the Spirituals to the American public and the world belongs to Fisk University. It was the famous Fisk Jubilee Singers that first made this country and Europe conscious of the beauty of these songs. The story of the struggles and successes of the Jubilee Singers, as told in the Fisk Collection of the Spirituals, reads like a romance. The first impetus upward was given them in New York under the powerful patronage of Henry Ward Beecher. With far-reaching wisdom Fisk University devoted itself to the careful collection and recording of the Spirituals, and so the work of the earlier collectors was broadened and improved upon. The work of Fisk University was quickly followed up by Hampton; Calhoun School, in Alabama; Atlanta University; Tuskegee Institute, and other schools in the South. These schools have for two generations been nurseries and homes for these songs.

Within the past ten or twelve years thorough musicians have undertaken a study of this music; a scientific study of it as folk music and an evaluation of its sociological as well as its musical importance. Chief among these is H. E. Krehbiel, more than thirty years music

47

PREFACE

critic on the New York Tribune. For many years Mr. Krehbiel made a study of Negro music, and gathered a vast amount of data. In 1914 he published his *Afro-American Folksongs,* which has already been referred to here. Shortly afterwards an excellent and sound book on the subject, *Folk Songs of the American Negro,* was published by Professor John W. Work of Fisk University. Natalie Curtis Burlin issued *The Hampton Series—Negro Folk-Songs,* in four parts containing the results of her investigations and studies at Hampton aided by phonograph records. Maud Cuney Hare of Boston contributed to the sum of historical and scientific knowledge regarding Negro music. A number of foreign musicians and observers, mostly Germans, have written on the same theme.

Today the Spirituals have a vogue. They are beyond the place where the public might hear them only through the quartets of Fisk or Hampton or Atlanta or Tuskegee. Today the public buys the Spirituals, takes them home and plays and sings them. This has been brought about because the songs have been put into a form that makes them available for singers and music lovers. The principal factor in reaching this stage has been H. T. Burleigh, the eminent colored musician and composer. Mr. Burleigh was the pioneer in making arrangements for the Spirituals that widened their appeal and extended their use to singers and the general musical public. Along with Mr. Burleigh and following him was a group of talented colored composers working to the same end: Nathaniel Dett, Carl Diton, J. Rosamond Johnson and N. Clark Smith. The vogue of the Spirituals was added to by the publishing of twenty-four piano arrangements of Spirituals by Coleridge-Taylor. Clarence Cameron White of Boston published a number of arrangements for violin and piano. There were others who aided greatly by organizing choruses and teaching them to sing these songs; foremost among whom were Mrs. Azalia Hackley, Mrs. Daisy Tapley and William C. Elkins. The latest impulse given to the spread of the Spirituals has come within the last year or two through their presentation to the public by colored singers on the concert stage. The superlatively fine rendition of these songs by Roland Hayes, Paul Robeson, Miss Marion Anderson, and Julius Bledsoe has brought them to their highest point of celebrity and

48

placed the classic stamp upon them. Today it is appropriate for any artist, however great, to program one or a group of these Spirituals.

A number of white persons aided in securing the general recognition which the Spirituals now enjoy. Several white musicians have made excellent arrangements for some of these songs. David Mannes, long interested in Negro music, was instrumental together with Mrs. Natalie Curtis Burlin, Mr. Elbridge Adams and others in founding a colored music school settlement in the Harlem section of New York City. Clement Wood, the poet, has for several years given lectures on the Spirituals, illustrated by voice and at the piano. Carl Van Vechten, whom I have quoted, has made a study of Negro music and has written a number of articles on the subject. But the present regard in which this Negro music is held is due overwhelmingly to the work of Negro composers, musicians and singers. It was through the work of these Negro artists that the colored people themselves were stirred to a realization of the true value of the Spirituals; and that result is more responsible for the new life which pulses through this music than any other single cause. I have said that these songs passed through a period when the front ranks of the Negro race would have been willing to let them die. Immediately following Emancipation those ranks revolted against everything connected with slavery, and among those things were the Spirituals. It became a sign of not being progressive or educated to sing them. This was a natural reaction, but, nevertheless, a sadly foolish one. It was left for the older generation to keep them alive by singing them at prayer meetings, class meetings, experience meetings and revivals, while the new choir with the organ and books of idiotic anthems held sway on Sundays. At this period gospel hymn-book agents reaped a harvest among colored churches in the South. Today this is all changed. There is hardly a choir among the largest and richest colored churches that does not make a specialty of singing the Spirituals. This reawakening of the Negro to the value and beauty of the Spirituals was the beginning of an entirely new phase of race consciousness. It marked a change in the attitude of the Negro himself toward his own art material; the turning of his gaze inward upon his own cultural resources. Neglect and ashamedness gave place to study and pride. All the other artistic activities of the Negro have been influenced.

There is also a change of attitude going on with regard to the Negro. The country may not yet be conscious of it, for it is only in the beginning. It is, nevertheless, momentous. America is beginning to see the Negro in a new light, or, rather, to see something new in the Negro. It is beginning to see in him the divine spark which may glow merely for the fanning. And so a colored man is soloist for the Boston Symphony Orchestra and the Philharmonic; a colored woman is soloist for the Philadelphia Symphony Orchestra and the Philharmonic; colored singers draw concert goers of the highest class; Negro poets and writers find entrée to all the most important magazines; Negro authors have their books accepted and put out by the leading publishers. And this change of attitude with regard to the Negro which is taking place is directly related to the Negro's change of attitude with regard to himself. It is new, and it is tremendously significant.

The collection here presented is not definitive, but we have striven to make it representative of this whole field of music, to give examples of every variety of Spiritual. There is still enough material new and old for another book like this, and, perhaps, even for another.

In the arrangements, Mr. Rosamond Johnson and Mr. Brown have been true not only to the best traditions of the melodies but also to form. No changes have been made in the form of songs. The only development has been in harmonizations, and these harmonizations have been kept true in character. And so an old-time Negro singer could sing any of the songs through without encountering any innovations that would interrupt him or throw him off. They have not been cut up or "opera-ated" upon. The arrangers have endeavored above all else to retain their primitive "swing."

This collection is offered with the hope that it will further endear these songs to those who love Spirituals, and will awaken an interest in many others.

GO DOWN MOSES

Arranged by J. Rosamond Johnson

To Walter Damrosch

Go down, Mos - es

'Way down in E - gypt land,_____ Tell ole

Pha - - raoh, To let my peo-ple go.

Go down, Mos - es, 'Way down in E - gypt land,

Tell ole ___ Pha - raoh, To let my peo - ple go. When

Is - rael was in E - gypts land:
spoke the Lord," bold Mos - es said;

Let my peo - ple
Let my peo - ple

go, Op - pressed so hard they could not stand,
go, If not I'll smite your first born dead,

52

'HEAV'N BOUN' SOLDIER

Arranged by J. Rosamond Johnson

Hold out yo' light you heav'n boun' sol-dier, Hold out yo' light you heav'n boun' sol-dier, Hold out yo' light you heav'n boun' sol-dier, Let yo' light shine a-roun' de world.

JOSHUA FIT DE BATTLE OB JERICO

Arranged by Lawrence Brown

To Paul and Eslanda Robeson

56

Josh-ua! (At de) bat-tle ob Jer-i-co. (Up to) (de walls) (ob)

Jer-i-co. He marched with spear in han' "Go blow dem ram horns"

(Josh-u-a) cried, "Kase de) (bat-tle) am (in my) (han'." (Den de)

lam' ram sheep horns be-gin to blow, trum-pets be-gin to soun'.

57

WE AM CLIM'IN' JACOB'S LADDER

Arranged by J. Rosamond Johnson

To "Ma" White

DIDN'T OLD PHARAOH GET LOS'?

Arranged by J. Rosamond Johnson

To Azalia Hackley

60

EXTRA VERSES

(Quite often several verses are sung before returning to the chorus)

3. De Lord said unto Moses—
   "Go unto Pharaoh now,
   For I have hardened Pharaoh's heart,
   To me he will not bow."
   Cho.—Didn't old Pharaoh get los', etc.

4. Den Moses an' Aaron,
   To Pharaoh did go,
   "Thus says de God of Israel,
   Let my people go."
   Cho.—Didn't, etc.

5. Old Pharaoh said, "Who is de Lord
   Dat I should him obey?"
   "His name it is Jehovah,
   For he hears his people pray."
   Cho.—Didn't, etc.

6. Hark! hear de children murmur,
   Dey cry aloud for bread,
   Down came de hidden manna,
   De hungry soldiers fed.
   Cho.—Didn't, etc.

7. Den Moses numbered Israel,
   Through all de land abroad,
   Sayin', "Children, do not murmur,
   But hear de word of God."
   Cho.—Didn't, etc.

8. Den Moses said to Israel,
   As dey stood along de Shore
   "Yo' enemies you see today,
   You'll never see no more."
   Cho.—Didn't, etc.

9. Den down came raging Pharaoh,
   Dat you may plainly see,
   Old Pharaoh an' his host
   Got los' in de Red Sea.
   Cho.—Didn't, etc.

10. Den men an' women an' children
    To Moses dey did flock;
    Dey cried aloud for water,
    An' Moses smote de rock.
    Cho.—Didn't, etc.

11. An' de Lord spoke to Moses,
    From Sinai's smoking top,
    Sayin', "Moses lead de people,
    Till I shall bid you stop."
    Cho.—Didn't, etc.

SWING LOW SWEET CHARIOT

Arranged by J. Rosamond Johnson

To Mrs. Arthur Curtiss James

look'd ov-er Jor-dan, an' what did I see, Comin' for to car-ry me home, A

band of an-gels com-in' af-ter me, Com-in' for to car-ry me home. O,

Swing low sweet char-i-ot,__ Com-in' for to car-ry me

home, Swing low sweet char-i-ot,__ Com-in' for to car-ry me

home, Com-in' for to car-ry me home.

63

UP ON DE MOUNTAIN

Arranged by J. Rosamond Johnson

Way up on de moun-tain, Lord!___ Moun - tain
One day Lord,___ one day Lord,___ Walk - in'

top,___ Lord! I heard God talk - in' Lord!
'long___ Lord, Wid hung down head___ Lord!

Chil - lun,___ de char - iot stop___ Lord!
Chil - lun,___ an ach - in' heart___ Lord!

LIT'LE DAVID PLAY ON YO' HARP

Arranged by J. Rosamond Johnson

To David Mannes

Lit'- le Dav-id play on yo' harp, Hal-le-lu, hal-le-

lu, Lit'- le Dav-id play on yo' harp, hal-le-lu.___ Lit'- le Dav-id play on yo'

harp, Hal-le-lu, hal-le-lu, Lit'-le Dav-id play on yo' harp, hal-le-lu.___ Lit'-le

Dav-id was a shep-herd boy,___ he kill'd Go-li-a an' shout-ed fo' joy___ Lit'le

quit 'till his work was done.___ Jos-hua was de son of Nun___ He nev-er would

quit 'till his work was done.___ Lit'-le Dav-id play on yo' harp, Hal-le-lu, hal-le-

lu, Lit'-le Dav-id play on yo' harp, hal-le-lu.___ Lit'-le Dav-id play on yo' harp, Hal-le-

lu, hal-le-lu, Lit'-le Dav-id play on yo' harp, hal-le-lu___ ja.___

67

DIE IN DE FIEL'

Arranged by J. Rosamond Johnson

To Mrs. Francis C. Barlow

Moderately Lively

Oh, what a you say, seek-ers, Oh, what a you say seek-ers, Oh,

what a you say, seek-ers, A - bout dat Gos-pel war. An'

what a you say, broth-ers, Oh, what a you say, broth-ers, Oh,

what a you say, broth-ers, A - bout dat Gos-pel war, An' I
will die ___ in de fiel', will die ___ in de fiel',
will die ___ in de fiel' I'm on my jour - ney
home   Sing it ov - ah I   home.

RIDE ON, MOSES

Arranged by J. Rosamond Johnson

Lead

I've been trav-lin' all de day, Ride on, Mo-ses To hear de good folks sing an' pray; I want to go home in de mawn-in' Dey pray'd so long I could not wait,

Ride on, Mo-ses, I know de Lord would pass dat way, I want to go home in de mawn-in' Den

Response

Ride on, ride on, ride on, Mo-ses Ride on,

repeat for verses   D.S.   *last time*

King E-man-u-al, I want to go home in de mawn-in'   want to go home in de mawn-in'

D.S.

70

ALL GOD'S CHILLUN GOT WINGS

Arranged by J. Rosamond Johnson

To Otto H. Kahn

With happy spirit

1. I got a robe, you got a robe, All o' God's Chil-lun got a robe.
2. I got a wings, you got a wings, All o' God's Chil-lun got a wings.

When I get to heab'n I'm goin' to put on my robe, I'm goin' to
When I get to heab'n I'm goin' to put on my wings, I'm goin' to

shout all ov - ah God's Heab'n,— Heab'n,— Heab'n,— Ev-'ry-bo-dy talk-in' 'bout
fly all ov - ah God's Heab'n,— Heab'n,— Heab'n,— Ev-'ry-bo-dy talk-in' 'bout

Back to Vamp for 2d V.

heab'n ain't goin' dere; Heab'n,—— Heab'n,—— I'm goin' to shout all ov - ah God's Heab'n.——
heab'n ain't goin' dere; Heab'n,—— Heab'n,—— I'm goin' to fly all ov - ah God's Heab'n.——

71

3. I got a harp, you got a harp, All o' God's Chil-lun got a harp, When I get to heab'n I'm goin' to take up my harp, I'm goin' to play all ov - ah God's Heab'n, ___ Heab'n, ___ Heab'n, ___ Ev-'y-bo-dy talk-in' 'bout heab'n ain't goin' dere, Heab'n ___ Heab'n ___ I'm goin' to play all ov - ah God's Heab'n.

I got shoes, you got shoes, All o' God's Chil-lun got

72

shoes   When I get to heab'n I'm goin' to   put on   my shoes, I'm goin' to

walk all ov   ah God's Heab'n, ___   Heab'n, ___   Heab'n, ___   Ev-'y bo dy talk in' 'bout

heab'n ain't goin' dere, Heab'n, ___   Heab'n ___ I'm goin' to walk all ov — ah God's

Heab'n ___   I'm goin' to walk all ov   ah God's Heab'n, ___ I'm goin' to walk all ov   ah God's Heab ___

— 'n, I'm goin' to walk all ov — ah, goin' to talk all ov — ah God's Heab — 'n.

a tempo   rit.   slower

DERE'S NO HIDIN' PLACE DOWN DERE

Arranged by Lawrence Brown

To Carl Van Vechten

Dere's no hid - in' place down dere, Dere's no hid - in' place down dere, Oh I went to de rock to hide my face, De rock cried out, "No hid-in' place," dere's no hid - in' place down dere. Oh de rock cried, "I'm burn - in' too," Oh de rock cried, "I'm burn - in'

too," Oh de rock cried out I'm burnin'too, I want a go to hebben as well as you, dere's

no hid - in'place down dere. Oh de sin-ner man he gamb-led an' fell, Oh de

sin-ner man he gambled, an' fell Oh de sin-ner man gambled, he gambled an'fell; he

wanted to go to hebben, but he had to go to hell dere's no hid-in'place down dere.

GIMME DAT OL'-TIME RELIGION

Arranged by J. Rosamond Johnson

Moderately lively

Gimme dat ol' - time re - ligion, gimme dat ol' time re - li-gion, gimme dat ol' - time re - li - gion,____ It's good e - nough for me. Jus' gimme dat ol' - time re - li-gion, gimme dat ol' - time re - li-gion, gimme dat ol' - time re - li - gion,____ It's

LIS'EN TO DE LAM'S

Arranged by J. Rosamond Johnson

To Mary Frances Vail

Lis-'en to de lam's, ___ all a - cry-in'. Lis-'en to de

lam's; ___ all a - cry-in'. Lis-'en to de lam's; ___ all a - cry - in' I

wan-ta go to hea-ben when I die. O, Lis-'en to de wan'-ta go to hea-ben when I die.

Come on sis-ter wid yo' ups an' downs, Wan'-ta go to hea-ben when I die. De
Come on mourn-er an'-a dont be shame, Wan'-ta go to hea-ben when I die. De
Mind out bro-ther how you walk de cross, Wan'-ta go to hea-ben when I die. Yo'

an-gel's wait-in' for to give you a crown, wan'-ta go to hea-ben when I die. O,
an-gel's wait-in' for to write-a yo' name, wan'-ta go to hea-ben when I die. O,
foot might slip-a an' yo' soul get-a los',

1. *omit after last verse*

2. wan'-ta go to hea-ben when I die. O, Lis-'en to de lam's;___ all a-cry-in' Lis-'en to de

lam's;___ all a-cry-in', Lis-'en to de lam's;___ all a-cry-in', I wan'-ta go to hea-ben when I

1. *omit after last verse*

D.S.§ *last time*   *little slower and softer*

die. wan'-ta go to hea-ben when I die.___ Lord, I wan'-ta go to hea-ben when I die.___

D.S.

little slower and softer

79

HE'S JUS' DE SAME TODAY

Arranged by J. Rosamond Johnson

sol - diers, __ f'om Egy-pt's lan' did flee, His en-e-mies were __ in be-
to his God, would not bow down __ to men, An' by God's en - e-my

hin' him, __ An' in front of him de sea. God raised de wa - ters
he was hurled in - to de li - on's den, God locked de li - on's

like a wall, An o-pened up de way, An' de God dat lived in
jaw we read, An' robbed him of his prey, An' de God dat lived in

Mo - ses' time is jus___ de same___ to - day.

Dan - iels' time is jus___ de same___ to - day. Is ___

RESPONSE

jus_____ de same to - day, ___ Jus'_____ de same to-day, ___ An' de

God dat _ lived in Mo - ses' time is jus' de same _ to - day.

Dan - iel's

molto ritard.

Repeat for Verses

D.S. 𝄋 *Last time*

When day. _____

D.S. 𝄋

81

STAN' STILL JORDAN

Arranged by J. Rosamond Johnson

To My Mother, Helen Louise Johnson

Stan' still ___ Jor - dan, Stan' still Jor - - dan.

Stan' still, Jor - dan, Lord, I can't stan' ___ still.

Jor - - dan riv - er, Jor dan riv - er,

Jor - - dan riv - er, is chil - ly and cold. ___

It will chill - a - my bod - y, It will chill - a - my bod - y,

It will chill - a - my bod - y, but not my soul.

Stan' still Jor - dan, Stan' still Jor - dan,

Stan' still Jor dan, Lord, I can't stan' still.

Dying out slowly

84

SOMEBODY'S KNOCKIN' AT YO' DO'

Arranged by J. Rosamond Johnson

To Samuel Coleridge-Taylor

85

PP REFRAIN *(Little slower)*

Some-bod-y's knock-in' at yo' do? Some-bod-y's knock-in' at yo' do.

O,____ sin-ner, why don't you an-swer? Some-bod-y's knock-in' at yo' do?

rit.

SINGIN' WID A SWORD IN MA HAN'

Arranged by J. Rosamond Johnson

To Azalia Hackley

(Melody by courtesy of Miss H. B. Lee, Palmer Memorial Institute, Sedalia, N. C.)

Moderately Slow

Sing-in' wid a sword in ma han', Lord,

Sing-in' wid a sword in ma han',

Sing-in' wid a sword in ma han', Lord,

Sing-in' wid a sword in ma han'. Pur-ti-est sing-in' ev-er I heard,'Way ov-ah on de
Pur-ti-est shout-in' ev-er I saw, 'Way ov-ah on de

hill, De an-gels sang an' I sang too, Sing-in' wid a sword in ma han', Lord,
hill, De an-gels shout an' I shout too, Shout-in' wid a sword in ma han', Lord,

Sing-in' wid a sword in ma han', in ma han', Lord, Sing-in' wid a sword in ma
Shout-in' wid a sword in ma han', in ma han', Lord, Shout-in' wid a sword in ma

han'. Sing-in' wid a sword in ma han', — Lord, Sing-in' wid a sword in ma
han'. Shout-in' wid a sword in ma han', — Lord, Shout-in' wid a sword in ma

87

han'.　Sing-in' wid a sword in ma　han',—Lord,　Sing-in' wid a sword in ma
han'.　Shout-in' wid a sword in ma　han',—Lord,　Shout-in' wid a sword in ma

han',　In ma han',　Lord,　Sing - in' wid a sword in ma han'.
han',　In ma han',　Lord,　Shout-in' wid a sword in ma han'.

D.C. % Fine

EXTRA VERSES

Purtiest preachin' ever I heard,
Way ovah on de hill,
De Angels preach'd an' I preach'd too,
Preachin' wid a sword in ma han', Lord,
Preachin' wid a sword in ma han', Lord,
Preachin' wid a sword in ma han'.

Purtiest prayin' ever I heard,
Way ovah on de hill,
De Angels pray'd an' I pray'd too,
Prayin' wid a sword in ma han', Lord,
Prayin' wid a sword in ma han', Lord,
Prayin' wid a sword in ma han'.

Purtiest mournin' ever I heard,
Way ovah on de hill,
De Angels mourn'd an' I mourn'd too,
Mournin' wid a sword in ma han', Lord,
Mournin' wid a sword in ma han', Lord,
Mournin' wid a sword in ma han'.

I COULDN'T HEAR NOBODY PRAY

Arranged by J. Rosamond Johnson

To W. E. Burghardt DuBois

Moderately slow (*with religious devotion*)

An' I could-n't hear no-bod-y pray, O, Lord, I could-n't hear no-bod-y pray, O, Lord, O, 'way down yon-der by my self an' I could-n't hear no-bod-y pray, In de val-ley, I could-n't hear no-bod-y pray. On a my knees — I could-n't hear no-bod-y pray. Wid my bur-den, I

89

pray, Hal-le-lu - jah. I could-n't hear no-bod-y pray. Troubles am o - ver I

could-n't hear no-bod-y pray In de King-dom I could-n't hear no-bod-y

pray, Wid a my Je - sus, I could-n't hear no-bod-y pray, O, Lord, An' I

could-n't hear no-bod-y pray, O, Lord, I could-n't hear no-bod-y pray, O, Lord, O

way down yon - der by my-self An' I could-n't hear no-bod-y pray.

rit gradually

91

MY WAY'S CLOUDY

Arranged by J. Rosamond Johnson

Sen' dem an-gels down, Dere's fire a-mong dem Me-tho-dis'__ Oh,
Sen' dem an-gels down, He missed de soul he thought he had,__ Oh,

sen'-a dem an-gels down Old__
sen'-a dem an-gels down. O, breth-er-en,

My__ way,__ my way's clou-dy, my__ way, Go

sen'-a dem an-gels down, O, breth-er-en down__

IT'S ME, O, LORD

Arranged by J. Rosamond Johnson

To Natalie Curtis Burlin

prayer, Tain't my mother or my fath-er but it's me O, Lord—
prayer, Tain't the deacon or my lead-er but it's me O, Lord—

Standin' in the need of prayer. Tain't the prayer. It's me, it's—me, it's
Standin' in the need of—

me O, Lord,— standin' in the need of prayer, It's me, it's me, it's

me O, Lord, An I'm stand-in' in the need of prayer.

95

I GOT A HOME IN-A DAT ROCK

Arranged by Lawrence Brown

To Walter and Gladys White

see? Poor man Laz-rus, poor as I, When he died he foun' a home on high. He had a

home in-a dat Rock, Don't you see? Rich man, Di - ves, He lived so well, Don't you

see? Rich man, Di - ves, He lived so well, Don't you see? Rich man,

rit.   *a tempo*

Di - ves, he lived so well, when he died he foun' a home in Hell, He had no

home in-a dat Rock, Don't you see? God gave Noah de Rain - bow sign, Don't you see? God gave Noah de Rain-bow sign, Don't you see? God gave Noah de Rain-bow sign, No mo

rit.

wa-ter but fire nex' time, Bet-ter get a home in-a dat Rock, Don't you see?

8va

BY AN' BY

Arranged by J. Rosamond Johnson

To Mrs. William Curtis Demorest

Lively

O, by an' by,—

by an' by — I'm gwinter lay down my heavy load.— O,

heavy load___ I know my robes gwinter fit me well,___
hell is deep an' a dark des - pair,___

I'm gwin-ter lay down my heavy load___ I tried it on at de
I'm gwin-ter lay down my heavy load___ O, stop po' sin - ner an'

gates of hell,___ I'm gwinter lay down my heavy load. O, heavy load. O,
don't go dere,·___ I'm gwinter lay down my

by an' by, by an' by, I'm gwinter lay down my heavy load. O, heavy load.

DEEP RIVER

Arranged by J. Rosamond Johnson

To Booker T. Washington

want to cross o - ver in - to camp - ground, — Lord, — I

pp slower and softer
want to cross o - ver in - to camp - ground.

Oh, — chil-lun, Oh, don't you want to go, — to that gos-pel feast, That

prom-ised land, that land, where all is peace?— Walk in-to heav-en, and

WHO DAT A-COMIN' OVAH YONDAH?

Arranged by J. Rosamond Johnson

ROLL JORDAN, ROLL

Arranged by J. Rosamond Johnson

To Paul Robeson

Roll Jor - dan, roll, Roll Jor - dan, roll, I want - er go to heav - 'n when I die,— To hear ol' Jor - dan roll. O, breth - er - en, O, sist - er - en, Roll Jor - dan

roll,   Roll Jor - dan, roll,   I

want - er go to heav - 'n when I die, To hear ol' Jor - dan roll. Oh

broth - ers you ought - er been dere,
sin - ner you ought - er been dere,   Yes my

Lord A - sit - tin' up in de king - dom, To

DE BLIN' MAN STOOD ON DE ROAD AN' CRIED

Arranged by J. Rosamond Johnson

To Sidney Woodward

108

ROLL DE OL' CHARIOT ALONG

Arranged by J. Rosamond Johnson

To Elbridge L. Adams

Roll de ol' cha-riot a-long, yes, roll de ol' cha-riot a-long, yes, Roll de ol' cha-riot a-long Ef yo don't hang on be-hin'. O Christ-ans, Roll de ol' Cha-riot a-long, yes, roll de ol' cha-riot a-long, yes, roll de ol' cha-riot a-long, Ef yo'dont hang on be-hin': Ef yo

Moth-er want to go She shall wear a star-ry crown, Ef yo'
Moth-er's in the way Jus' roll right over, Ef yo'

moth-er want to go She shall wear a star-ry crown, Ef yo' moth-er want to go She shall
moth-er's in the way Jus' roll right over, Ef yo' moth-er's in the way Jus'

wear a star-ry crown, An' she must hang on be-hin': O Chris-tians,
roll right over, An' yo must hang on be-hin':

Roll de ol' cha-riot a-long, yes, roll de ol' cha-riot a-long, yes,

Repeat for Verse   *Last Time*

Roll de ol' cha-riot a-long, Ef yo' don't hang on be-hin'. Ef yo' hin'.

CALVARY

Arranged by J. Rosamond Johnson

To my Father, James Johnson

112

113

STEAL AWAY TO JESUS

Arranged by J. Rosamond Johnson

To Roland Hayes

Je - sus! Steal a - way, steal a - way home, I

aint got long to stay here. My Lord, He calls me, He

calls me by the thun - der, The trum - pet sounds with -

in - a my soul, I aint got long to stay here.

Steal a-way, steal a-way, steal a-way to Je - sus!

Steal a-way, steal a-way home I ain't got long to stay here.

Steal a-way, steal a-way, steal a-way to

Je - sus! Steal a-way, steal a-way home, I

116

GWINE UP

Arranged by J. Rosamond Johnson

To Percy Grainger

Moderately Lively (*with steady rhythm*)

Oh, yes, I'm gwine up, gwine up, gwine all de way, Lord Gwine up, gwine up to see de hea-ben-ly lan'. Oh, yes, I'm lan'. Oh, —

Saints an' sin-ners will-a you go, gwine to keep-a clim-in' high,

See de hea-ben-ly lan', I'm-a gwine up to heab'n fo' to see my robe,
See de hea-ben-ly lan', Till I meet dem-a an-gels in-a de sky,

See de hea-ben-ly lan';— Gwine to see my robe an' try it on,
See de hea-ben-ly lan';— Dem-a snow white an-gels I. shall see,

See de hea-ben-ly lan',— It am bright-er dan-a dat___ glit-ter-in' sun,
See de hea-ben-ly lan',— Den de deb-bil am-a gwine to let-'a me be,

See de hea-ben-ly lan'. Oh, yes, I'm Gwine up, gwine up,
See de hea-ben-ly lan'. Oh, yes, I'm

gwine all de way, Lord, Gwine up gwine up to

1.
D.C. to 𝄋 | *Last time*
see de hea-ben-ly lan'.— see de hea-ben-ly lan'.___

D.C. to 𝄋

119

I'M TROUBLED IN MIND

Arranged by J. Rosamond Johnson

O, GAMBLER, GIT UP OFF O' YO' KNEES

Arranged by J. Rosamond Johnson

Slowly with steady rhythm

122

MY LORD'S A-WRITIN' ALL DE TIME

Arranged by J. Rosamond Johnson

To Louis Graveure

Come down, come down, my Lord, come down,
Je - sus rides in de mid-dle of de 'air,

My Lord's a-writ-in' all de time, An' take me up to
My Lord's a-writ-in' all de time, He's call-in' sin-ners from

wear de crown, My Lord's a-writ-in' all de time. King
ev' - ry where, My Lord's a-writ-in' all de time. Oh, He

Chorus

sees all you do, He hears all you say,— My Lord's a-writ-in' all de time. Oh, He

sees all you do, He hears all you say,— My Lord's a-writ-in' all de time. Oh, He time. When

LEAD   RESPONSE

I was down in E - gypt's lan'— My Lord's a-writ-in' all de
Christ-ians, you had bet - ter pray,— My Lord's a-writ-in' all de

time, I heard some talk of de prom - ised lan',—
time, For Sa - tan's round you ev' - ry day,—

My Lord's a-writ-in' all de time. Oh,
My Lord's a-writ-in' all de _____ time. Oh, He

Chorus

sees all you do, He hears all you say, __ My Lord's a-writ-in' all de

time Oh, He sees all you do, He hears all you say, __

My Lord's a-writ-in' all de time yes, all de time.

GIT ON BOARD, LITTLE CHILLEN

Arranged by Lawrence Brown

To Laura J. Heathfield

board, lit-tle chil-len, Dere's room for ma-ny a mo', De fare is cheap, an' all can go, De

rich an' poor are dere,— No sec-ond class a-board dis train, No

diff-runce in de fare. Git on board, lit-tle chil-len, Git on board, lit-tle chil-len, Git on

board, lit-tle chil-len, Dere's room for ma-ny a mo'._____

GWINTER SING ALL ALONG DE WAY

Arranged by J. Rosamond Johnson

WHO'LL BE A WITNESS FOR MY LORD?

Arranged by J. Rosamond Johnson

To Carl Van Vechten

My soul is a wit-ness for my Lord, My soul is a wit-ness for my Lord, My

soul is a wit-ness for my Lord, My soul is a wit-ness for my Lord. You

read in de Bi-ble an' you un-der-stan', Me-thu-se-lah was de old-es' man, He

lived nine-hun-dred an' six-ty nine, He died an' went to heav-en, Lord, in-a due time. O, Me-thuse-lah was a wit - ness for my Lord, Me - thuse-lah was a wit - ness for my Lord, Me

thuse-lah was a wit - ness for my Lord, Me - thuse-lah was a wit - ness for my Lord. You

Lead

read in de Bib-le an' you un-der - stan', Sam-son was de strong-est man; Sam-son went out

at - a one time, An' he killed a-bout a thous-an' of de Phil-is - tine. De - li - lah fooled Sam-son,

dis-a we know, For de Hol - y Bib-le tells us so, She shaved off his head jus' as

131

clean as yo' han', An' his strength be-came de same as an - y natch'- al man. O,

Response

Sam-son was a wit - ness for my Lord, O, Sam-son was a wit - ness for my Lord, O,

Sam-son was a wit-ness for my Lord, O, Sam-son was a wit - ness for my Lord. Now

Lead

Dan - iel was a He - brew child, He went to pray to his God a - while, De

king at once for Dan-iel did sen', An' he put him right down in de lion-'s den;

132

133

KEEP A-INCHIN' ALONG

Arranged by J. Rosamond Johnson

To John W. Work

died one time gwine-ter die_ no mo' Mas-sa Je-sus is com-in' bye an' bye. O, I,
you in de Lord and de Lord in you, Mas-sa Je-sus is com-in' bye an' bye. O_
can I die when I'm in_ de Lord? Mas-sa Je-sus is com-in' bye an' bye. How

died one time gwine-ter die_ no mo' Mas-sa Je-sus is com-in' bye an' bye.
you in de Lord and de Lord in you, Mas-sa Je-sus is com-in' bye an' bye. Keep a-
can I die when I'm in_ de Lord? Mas-sa Je-sus is com-in' bye an' bye.

in-chin' a-long, Keep a-in-chin' a-long, Massa Je-sus is com-in' bye an' bye. Keep a-

Repeat for Verses

last time

in-chin' a-long like a po' inch worm, Mas-sa Je-sus is com-in' bye an' bye. O, bye.
How

135

WHERE SHALL I BE WHEN DE FIRS' TRUMPET SOUN'?

Arranged by J. Rosamond Johnson

PETER, GO RING DEM BELLS

Arranged by J. Rosamond Johnson

To "Singing" Johnson

heard fom heav'n to-day, I heard fom heav'n to-day, It's good news an' I

thank God too, I heard fom heav'n to-day. Oh, Pe-ter, go ring dem bells,

Pe-ter, go ring dem bells, Pe-ter, go ring dem bells I heard fom heav'n to-

day, I heard fom heav'n to-day.

139

NOBODY KNOWS DE TROUBLE I SEE

Arranged by J. Rosamond Johnson

To Henry E. Krehbiel

(*Note: This is a rare version.*)

pray for me, Broth-ers will you pray for me An'
Moth-ers

Repeat verses ad lib. D.S. 𝄋 *After last verse only*

help me to drive ole Sa-tan a- way. No-bod - y knows de

D.S.
pp

trouble I see, Lord, No-bod - y knows de trouble I see, No-bod - y

knows de trouble I see, Lord, No-bod - y knows like Je - sus.

141

EV'RY TIME I FEEL DE SPIRIT

Arranged by J. Rosamond Johnson

To Walter F. White

Moderately Slow

Ev'- ry time I feel de spir - it, move - in' in my heart, I will pray. O, ev'- ry time I feel de spir - it, move - in' in my heart, I will pray. (1)Up-on de

moun - tain _____ my Lord, spoke, _____ Out o' his mouth came _____
roun' me _____ look so shine, _____ Ask-a my Lord, if _____
riv - er _____ chill - y, cold, _____ Chill-a de bo - dy

143

FATHER ABRAHAM

Arranged by J. Rosamond Johnson

To Daisy Tapley

I'M A-ROLLIN'

Arranged by J. Rosamond Johnson

To Robert Edmond Jones

145

help me in de ser-vice of de Lord.___ I'm a-

roll - in', I'm a - roll - in', I'm a - roll-in', through an un-

friend - ly worl' I'm a - roll - in', I'm a -

roll - in', through an un - friend - ly worl'. *D. S. al Fine.*

D. S. al Fine.

147

DIDN'T MY LORD DELIVER DANIEL?

Arranged by J. Rosamond Johnson

To Robert Russa Moton

Set my foot on de Gos-pel ship, an' de ship be-gin to __ sail, It land-ed me o-ver on Can-aan's shore An' I'll nev-er come back no mo'. Did-n't my Lord de-liv-er Dan-iel, __ de-liv-er Dan-iel, __ de-liv-er Dan-iel, __ Did-n't my Lord de-liv-er Dan-iel __ An' why not-a ev-e-ry man.

O, WASN'T DAT A WIDE RIVER?

Arranged by J. Rosamond Johnson

152

river of Jor - dan is so wide, One mo' riv-er to cross. I
Sat- an am noth-in' but a snake in de grass, One mo' riv-er to cross. If

don't know how to get on de oth - er side; One mo' riv - er to
you aint might - y care - ful he will hol' you fas'; One mo' riv - er to

cross. Ol' cross. O, was-n't dat a wide riv - er, dat riv - er of Jor-dan, Lord,

Wide____ riv - er! Dere's one mo' riv - er to cross.____

KEEP ME F'OM SINKIN' DOWN

Arranged by J. Rosamond Johnson

tell you what I mean to do; Keep me f'om sink-in' down: I
look up yon-dah an' what do I see; Keep me f'om sink-in' down. I

mean to go to hea-v'n too; Keep me f'om sink-in' down I
see de an-gels beck-on-in' me, Keep me f'om sink-in' down.

Oh;— Lord,— Oh,— my Lord! Oh,— my good Lord!

Keep me f'om sink-in' down— f'om sink-in' down.

DE BAND O' GIDEON

Arranged by J. Rosamond Johnson

Lively

Oh, de band o' Gide - on, band o' Gide - on,
milk white hors - es, milk white hors - es,

band o' Gide - on ov - er in Jor - dan, Band o' Gide - on, band o' Gide - on
milk white hors - es ov - er in Jor - dan, Milk white hors - es, milk white hors - es

how I long___ to see dat day. Oh, de
how I long___ to see dat day. I

hail to my sis - ter, my sis - ter she bow low, Say, don't you want to
hail to dat mour - ner, dat mour - ner he bow low, Say, don't you want to

go to heav'n How I long to see dat day. I
go to heav'n How I long to see dat day. Oh, de

twelve white hors - es, twelve white hors - es, twelve white hors - es
hitch 'em to de char - - ot, hitch 'em to de char - i - ot, hitch 'em to de char - i - ot

ov - er in Jor - dan, Twelve white hors - es, twelve white hors - es, How I long to
ov - er in Jor - dan, Hitch 'em to de char - i - ot, hitch 'em to de char - i - ot How I long to

see dat day. Gwine to see dat day, To see dat day.

JOHN SAW THE HOLY NUMBER

Arranged by J. Rosamond Johnson

158

Worth - y worth - y is the Lamb, Sit - ting on the gold - en
Weep - ing Ma - ry weeps no more, Sit - ting on the gold - en

al - tar, Oh, al - tar John saw, Oh, John saw,

John saw the ho - ly num - ber sit - ting on the gold - en

al - tar al - tar On the gold - en al - tar

repeat pp *Last time*

mf - pp

rit.
dying away softly

GIVE ME JESUS

Arranged by J. Rosamond Johnson

MY LORD, WHAT A MORNIN'

Arranged by J. Rosamond Johnson

To Mary E. Floyd

(The title of this song has at times been erroneously printed "My Lord, What A Mourning")

hear de trum - pet sound,
hear de sin - ner moan, To wake de na - tions un - der ground,
hear de Christ - ians shout,

Look - in' to my God's right hand, When de stars be - gin to fall. My Lord, what a

morn - in', My Lord, what a morn - in', My Lord, what a morn - in', When de

stars be - gin to fall, When de stars be - gin to fall. _____

Repeat for Verses | *Last time*

② You'll
③ You'll

O, ROCKS DON'T FALL ON ME

Arranged by J. Rosamond Johnson

look o-vah yon-dah on Je-ri-cho's walls, Rocks__ an' moun-tains don't fall on me, An'
ey-ah-ry star re-fus-es to shine Rocks an' moun-tains don't fall on me, I

see dem sin-ners trem-ble an' fall,__ Rocks__ an' moun-tains don't fall on me. O,
know dat King Je-sus will-a be mine,__ Rocks__ an' moun-tains don't fall on me. De

in-a dat great great judg-a-ment day, Rocks__ an' moun-tains don't fall on me, De
trum-pet shall soun' An' de dead shall rise, Rocks__ an' moun-tains don't fall on me, An'

sin-ners will run to de rocks an say__ Rocks__ an' moun-tains don't fall on me.
go to de man-sions in-a de skies,__ Rocks__ an' moun-tains don't fall on me.

O, rocks, don't fall on me, O, rocks, don't fall on me, ___

O, rocks, don't fall on me, Rocks ___ an' moun-tains don't fall on me, I'm praying,

O, rocks, don't fall on me, O, rocks, don't fall on me, ___ O, rocks, don't

fall on me, Rocks ___ an' moun-tains don't fall on me, When fall on me.

Repeat for 2nd Verse. D.S. 𝄋 last time

D.S. 𝄋

166

DONE FOUN' MY LOS' SHEEP

Arranged by J. Rosamond Johnson

To H. T. Burleigh

That jes lef' Him nine-ty-nine, Go to de wild-er-ness, seek an' fin', Ef you fin' him,

bring him back, Cross de shoul-ders, Cross yo' back; Tell de neigh-bors all a-roun',

Dat los' sheep has done be foun: Done foun' my los' sheep,— Done foun' my los'

sheep,— Done foun' my los' sheep. In dat Res - sur - rec - tion Day sin-ner can't fin no hid-in' place, Go to de moun-tain, de moun-tain move;

Run to de hill, de hill run too. Sin-ner man trab-lin' on tremb-ling groun', Po' los' sheep aint

neb-ber been foun' Sin-ner why don't yo' stop and pray, Den you'd hear de Shep-herd say, Done

foun' my los' sheep, Done foun' my los' sheep, Done foun' my los' sheep.

169

WHAT YO' GWINE TO DO WHEN YO' LAMP BURN DOWN?

Arranged by J. Rosamond Johnson

Slowly with meditation

O,— po' sin-ner, O,— now is yo' time,— O,— po' sin-ner, O,— What yo' gwine to do when yo' lamp burn down

Fin' de Eas', fin' de Wes', What yo' gwine to do when yo' lamp burn down.
Head got wet wid de mid-night dew, What yo' gwine to do when yo' lamp burn down.

Fire gwine to burn down de wil-der-ness, What yo' gwine to do when yo' lamp burn down.
Morn-in'— star was a wit-ness too, What yo' gwine to do when yo' lamp burn down.

170

O,— po' sin-ner, O,— now is yo' time,— O,— po' sin-ner, O,—

What yo' gwine to do when yo' lamp burn down. Dey whipp'd Him up an dey whipp'd Him down,
Dey nail'd His han' an dey nail'd His feet,

Fine

What yo' gwine to do when yo' lamp burn down. Dey whipp'd dat man all
What yo' gwine to do when yo' lamp burn down. De ham-mer was heard on Je-

o - vah town, What yo' gwine to do when yo' lamp burn down.
rus - a - lem street, What yo' gwine to do when yo' lamp burn down.

D.S. %

HALLELUJAH!

Arranged by J. Rosamond Johnson

Hal - le - lu - jah! an' a hal - le - lu - jah!_ Hal - le - lu - jah, Lord! I been down in - to the sea. to the sea. O, I've

been to the sea an' I've done been tried, ___ Been down into the sea; O, I've
Christians, ___ Can't you ___ rise an' tell; ___ Been down into the sea; The ___
you don't ___ b'lieve I've ___ been re-deemed, Been down into the sea; Just ___
born of ___ God, I ___ know I am, ___ Been down into the sea; I'm ___

repeat verses ad lib. 2

been to the sea an' I've been bap-tize', ___ Been down into the sea. O, ___
glo-ries ___ of Im-man-u-el? ___ Been down into the sea. If, ___
watch my ___ face for the gos-pel gleam, ___ Been down into the sea. I'm ___
pur-chased by the ___ dy-ing Lamb, ___ Been down in ___ -to the sea.

Hal - le - lu-jah an' a hal - le ___ lu-jah ___

1 | 2 *Last time*

Hal-le - lu-jah, Lord ___ I've been down ___ in-to the sea. -to the sea.

173

CRUCIFIXION

Arranged by J. Rosamond Johnson

To Roland Hayes

They cru-ci-fied my Lord, an' He nev-er said a mum-ba-lin' word; They cru-ci-fied my Lord, an' He nev-er said a mum-ba-lin' word. Not a word, not a word, not a word. They nailed him to the tree, 'an He nev-er said a mum-ba-lin' word; They nailed him to the

174

tree, an' He nev-er said a mum-ba-lin' word. Not a word, not a word, not a word. They

little slower

pierced him in the side, an' He nev-er said a mum-ba-lin' word, They pierced him in the

f tempo

side, an' He nev-er said a mum-ba-lin' word. Not a word, not a word, not a word._____ The

little slower

blood came twink-lin' down, an' He nev-er said a mum-ba-lin' word; The blood came twink-lin'

Viol. Ob.

mf tempo

175

down,   an' He nev-er said a mum-ba-lin' word.   Not a   word,   not a

gradually growing softer and slower

word, not a word _____   He bow'd his head an' died,   an' He

pp   *f tempo*   *pp*

nev-er said a mum-ba-lin' word,   He bow'd his head an' died,   an' He

nev-er said a mum-ba-lin' word;   Not a   word, not a   word, not a   word. ___

gradually slower and softly dying away
r.h.   *r.h.*   *r.h.*
l.h.   *l.h.*   *ppp*

UNTIL I REACH-A MA HOME

Arranged by J. Rosamond Johnson

some say gim-me sil-vah, an' some say gim-me gol', But

I say gim-me Je-sus mos' pre-cious to ma soul. Dey

say dat John de Bap-tis' was noth-in' but a Jew, But de

ho-ly Bi-ble tells us, Dat he was a preach-er too. O, broth-ers,
O, sis-ters, Un-

til I reach - a ma home,_____ Un-

til I reach - a ma home._____ I

nev-ah in-ten' to give de jour-ney ov-ah, un-

til I reach ma home._____

179

I DONE DONE WHAT YA' TOL' ME TO DO

Arranged by J. Rosamond Johnson

To Clarence B. Ashenden

So glad __ I done done, So glad __ I done done, So __ glad __ I done done, __ I done

done - a what ya' tol' me to do. So __ glad __ I done done, So glad __ I done done, So __

glad __ I done done, __ I done done - a what ya' tol' me to do. Tol' me to

pray, an' I done pray, tol' me to pray an' I done __ pray, So __ glad __ I done done, __ I done

done-a what ya' tol' me to do. So glad__ I done done, So glad__ I done done So
(After last verse only) Thank God__ I done done, Thank God__ I done done Thank

Ending for all verses. | *Last ending*

glad I done done, I done done a-what ya' tol' me to do. Tol' me to done a-what ya' tol' me to do.
God I done done,

YOU MAY BURY ME IN DE EAS'

Arranged by Lawrence Brown

To Alec Rowley

Lento

You may bur - y me in de Eas', You may

bur-y me in de Wes', But I'll hear de trump-et soun'__ in dat morn - in', In dat

YOU GOT A RIGHT

Arranged by J. Rosamond Johnson

God in de heav'n gwin-ter ans-wer prayer (O bre-ther-en)
(O sis-ter-en)

You got a right, I got a right, We all got a right to de tree of life Yes, tree of life.

WEARY TRAVELER

Arranged by J. Rosamond Johnson

To John McCormack

Slowly *(with steady swing)*

mf

Let us

cheer the wea-ry trav-el-er, _____ Cheer the wea-ry trav-el-er: Let us

cheer the wea-ry trav-el-er, A - long the heav-en-ly way O, let us

cheer the wea-ry trav-el-er, _____ Cheer the wea-ry trav-el-er; Let us

cheer the wea-ry trav-el-er, A - long the heav-en-ly way. I'll

take my gos-pel trum - pet, An' I'll be-gin __ to
if you meet with cross - es, An' tri - als on __ the

blow, An' if my Sav - iour helps me, I'll
way,) Just keep your trust in Je - sus, An'

blow wher - ev - er I go; An' broth - ers, pray. Let us
don't for - get __ to

cheer the wea - ry trav - el - er, __

Cheer the wea - ry trav - el - er; Let us cheer the wea - ry trav - el - er, A - long the heav - en - ly way.